Of Psalms and Songs and Poetry

Of Psalms and Songs and Poetry

Johannes W. H. van der Bijl
Foreword by Phil Knox

RESOURCE *Publications* • Eugene, Oregon

OF PSALMS AND SONGS AND POETRY

Copyright © 2025 Johannes W. H. van der Bijl. All rights reserved. Except for brief quotations in critical publications or reviews, no part of this book may be reproduced in any manner without prior written permission from the publisher. Write: Permissions, Wipf and Stock Publishers, 199 W. 8th Ave., Suite 3, Eugene, OR 97401.

Resource Publications
An Imprint of Wipf and Stock Publishers
199 W. 8th Ave., Suite 3
Eugene, OR 97401

www.wipfandstock.com

PAPERBACK ISBN: 979-8-3852-5202-2
HARDCOVER ISBN: 979-8-3852-5203-9
EBOOK ISBN: 979-8-3852-5204-6
VERSION NUMBER 07/11/25

Scripture quotations are from The ESV® Bible (The Holy Bible, English Standard Version®) © 2001 by Crossway, a publishing ministry of Good News Publishers. Used by permission. All rights reserved.

Dedicated to the Society of Anglican Missionaries and Senders.
To our missionaries, senders, and staff,
many of whom discovered that the presence of God
is most clearly defined in the darkest valleys of life.

Contents

Foreword by Phil Knox | ix
Preface | xi

Book One: Psalms 1–41 | 1
Book Two: Psalms 42–72 | 57
Book Three: Psalms 73–89 | 99
Book Four: Psalms 90–106 | 129
Book Five: Psalms 107–150 | 151
Songs | 219
Poetry | 251

Bibliography | 273

Foreword

THE PSALMS HAVE ALWAYS occupied a unique place in the life of the church. They are both ancient and startlingly contemporary, liturgical and deeply personal, theological yet unflinchingly emotional. In the Psalms, we encounter humanity in all its vulnerability, crying out, repenting, rejoicing, remembering, and worshiping, and we encounter God in all his steadfastness, holiness, mercy, and majesty. It is no wonder that the Psalter has shaped the worship, prayer, and poetic imagination of believers for centuries.

Yet each generation must learn to sing the Psalms afresh. While the Hebrew poetry of Scripture remains unchanging, its resonances shift with time, language, and culture. In *Of Psalms and Songs and Poetry*, the reader is invited into a fresh engagement with these ancient songs through a collection of poems that echo, refract, and reembody the voices of the psalmists for today's world.

What distinguishes this volume is its rare combination of reverent faithfulness and creative originality. The author does not merely paraphrase or retranslate the Psalms, he inhabits them. Each poem emerges from a deep wrestling with the text, shaped by both theological insight and lived experience. These are not academic exercises nor sentimental meditations; they are true spiritual songs, written in the tradition of those who have long sung their way through suffering, pilgrimage, silence, praise, and perplexity.

Theologically, the poems are grounded. There is no flattening of the biblical witness here, no easy harmonizing of lament into praise or complexity into cliché. Instead, the poetic voice is allowed to retain its full biblical range: from the groanings of the forsaken to the exultations of the redeemed; from the anguished cry for justice to the still repose of trust. The result is a book that not only reflects the contours of the Psalms but deepens our capacity to read them with integrity.

Foreword

Literarily, the work is beautifully crafted. The language is lyrical without being overwrought, modern without being casual, and poetic without being obscure. There is a rhythmic attentiveness throughout that makes many of these poems suitable for liturgical use, public reading, or musical adaptation—yet they also reward quiet, personal reflection. One hears in them echoes of the great hymnists, the mystics, and the modern lyric poets, yet the voice remains distinctive and fresh.

Devotionally, the book offers a gift to the Church. In an age where much of contemporary worship risks being either emotionally shallow or theologically thin, these poems stand as a call back to the deep well of biblical spirituality. They invite the reader not only to read but to pray, to weep, to sing, and to hope. They offer words to those who have lost theirs, and they stir longing in those who have grown tired or dry. In short, they do what true psalm-inspired poetry should do: they draw us back to God.

I commend *Of Psalms and Songs and Poetry* to pastors, worship leaders, poets, and all who long to hear, and speak, the voice of faith in this present age. May these poems serve as both echo and invitation: echoing the voice of the ancient psalmists, and inviting us into the living song of God's people in every generation.

Phil Knox
Author, missiologist, evangelist, and award-winning poet
Evangelical Alliance UK

Preface

WHAT BEGAN AS A Lenten discipline has grown into the book you now hold. My initial intention was simple and devotional: to read through the Psalms prayerfully, accompanied by a trusted commentary, and respond by crafting hymns and songs suitable for congregational worship. The early pieces reflect this purpose—lyrical, liturgical, and shaped for communal voice. Sadly, I'm no musician, and this Gilbert is still looking for his Sullivan.

But as the days passed and the Psalms unfolded, something deeper began to take place. These ancient songs, so rich with lament, praise, protest, and hope, began to echo not just the inner life of a distant writer, but the anguish and longing of our own time. In the psalmist's cries, I began to hear the cries of today's world—of believers living amid war, political turmoil, displacement, self-centered indifference, and uncertainty. And within that resonance, I found my own voice shifting.

What had begun as a discipline of interpretation and songwriting became something far more personal. My writing moved beyond liturgical form into a more intimate dialogue—between the ancient text and the contemporary soul, between history and heartache, between the sacred and the suffering.

While many of these pieces remain musical and may yet be sung, they carry a different weight now. They are prayers shaped not only by study, but by solidarity—poems born at the intersection of Scripture and the struggles of the present age. If these offerings can help others hear the voice of the Psalms more clearly in their own wilderness, then the journey will have been worth it.

Johannes W. H. van der Bijl
De Kuilenaar, Heiloo
The Netherlands

BOOK ONE

Psalms 1–41

PSALM 1: BLESSED

Blessed is the one who walks in the way, avoiding the paths that lead us astray. Delighting in truth—the Law of the Lord—learning and living in step with his word.

Chorus
Like trees by the waters, steadfast and strong, bearing their fruit all the year long. The righteous shall flourish, their hope ever sure, rooted in Jesus their lives are secure.

Delight in the word and live in its light; meditate on it by both day and night. Like trees in the river of life will mature, those who walk in the way of the Lord will endure.

Not so the wicked, like chaff they are blown, their ways are unstable, they stand all alone.
The Lord watches over the righteous with care, but the paths of the wicked lead to despair.

Chorus

Blessed is the one who trusts in his name, who walks in his truth, forever the same.
Firm in our faith, we'll grow by his grace, with joy in his presence, his loving embrace.

O teach us, dear Lord, to walk in your light, to shun what is wrong, to cling to what's right.
Our joy is in Jesus, our Savior, our guide, we boldly move forward with you by our side.

Chorus

PSALM 2: FOR EVERY NATION, GOD IS KING

Chorus
For every nation, God is King, he sits enthroned above all things.
Through every tribe, let praise ascend, and every knee before him bend.

O Sovereign Lord, Creator wise, you formed the earth, the seas, the skies,
Your mighty hand no foe withstands, your gospel spreads to distant lands.
As Peter prayed with steadfast might, send boldness, Lord, and holy light.
Proclaim through us the Savior's name and spread abroad his glorious fame.

Our Lord commands us, don't be still, disciple nations, teach his will.
All power's his, on earth, in heav'n, so, rise and speak the word he's given.
Though nations rage and plots unfurl, our Lord has overcome the world.
Take heart, O Church, we will not fail, the gates of hell will not prevail.

Chorus

No evil weapon shall succeed, this is the word our Lord decreed.
We press on in the race we run, we fight the fight till day is done.
By faith we stand, the crown awaits, our Lord has opened heaven's gates.
Through Abraham's seed the promise flows, till every nation Jesus knows.

Our war is not with human beings, but rulers dark and powers unseen.
With armor bright, the gospel shod, we march as victors through our God.
The Spirit moves, the nations hear the Father's answer to Christ's prayer,
That all the earth his own will be, his heritage perpetually.

Chorus

May nations bless the Lord above, as he embraces them in love.
May all rebellion, small or great, before the throne disintegrate.

Send us as servants of your Son; your kingdom come, your will be done.
Till every tongue and heart's confessed, and hell itself is dispossessed.

Chorus

Also based on Genesis 12:3; Isaiah 54:17; Matthew 28:18–20; John 16:33; Acts 4:24–31; Ephesians 6:12; and 2 Timothy 4:7–8.

PSALM 3: SHIELD OF THE FAITHFUL

Chorus
O Shield of the faithful, our strength and our might,
You rescue the lowly, you banish the night.
O God the Almighty, our refuge, our song,
Though trials are many, we shall overcome.

As agents of darkness, my enemies rise,
They mock and they whisper, they seek my demise.
But you are my glory, you lift up my head,
And hear all my prayers both silent and said.

Chorus

I cry to the Lord, from his throne he replies,
His voice shakes the heavens, my foes he defies.
I lay down to rest, and I wake in his care,
Though thousands surround me, I will not despair.

Chorus

Arise, O my God, and hear our request,
Deliver your people, set free the oppressed.
Salvation belongs to the Lord ever true,
Your blessings sustain us; our trust is in you.

Chorus and Outro
Though trials are many, we shall overcome,
For you are our refuge, our shield, and our song.

PSALM 4: O GOD OF GRACE

O God, you are my righteousness, I lift my voice to you.
In darkest night, your mercy shines, relieves and makes me new.
How long will I be put to shame by those who love what's vain?
But know the Lord has set apart the faithful for his name.

Chorus
O God of grace, in you I rest, you hear me when I speak.
Shine on me with your radiant love and lift me when I'm weak.

When anger stirs and doubts arise, let sin not take control.
In quiet trust, in silent awe, I yield to you my soul.
The world may chase its fleeting joys, its riches and acclaim.
But I have found my greatest joy, I will not be ashamed.

Chorus

Bridge
You have filled my heart with joy, more than abundance brings.
And in your peace I safely rest, beneath your shadowed wings.

O God of righteousness and peace, you hear me when I call.
Through trials deep your hand upholds, and so, I will not fall.
Grant us, O Lord, your holy joy, your truth to light our way.
And let all lives and every voice be lifted up in praise.

Chorus and Outro
O Lord, you are my solid rock, relief in my distress.
In you I know I'm safe and still, in you I know I'm blessed.

PSALM 5: LIFT US AND LEAD US

O Lord, in the morning I lift up my voice;
Consider my groaning, and let me rejoice.
My King and my Savior, my Master and Lord,
I wait and I ponder and rest on your word.

Chorus
O God, in your mercy and loving embrace,
Great and abundant your goodness and grace.
Lift us and lead us to walk in your way,
For you are our refuge, our strength, and our stay.

You do not delight in the wicked or wrong;
The proud and the haughty can never belong.
Lies and deceit you abhor and disdain;
You hate what is evil and all that is vain.

Chorus

Though many approach me with flattering words,
Their speech and their counsel is rendered absurd,
For grave and destruction and absence of truth
Will cause them to fall in the prime of their youth.

Chorus

Bridge
Let all who trust in you rejoice and let them sing with cheerful voice.
Protect the ones who love your name and keep them safe in your domain.

Chorus

PSALM 6: TURN, O LORD, DELIVER MY LIFE

Chorus
Turn, O Lord, deliver my life, save me for your mercy's sake.
O let me live so I might sing praise to you when I awake.

Do not be angry with me Lord, severity I fear.
Be gracious, I am languishing, but you, O Lord, are near.

Chorus

I soak my bed with tears each night, I groan in my despair.
Yet you are kind, compassionate, your love beyond compare.

Chorus

Bridge
Away from me, my enemies, the Lord accepts my plea.
He answers me for I am his, and he has set me free.

Chorus and Outro
To the broken, Lord, be merciful; to the weary, grant them rest.
Your steadfast love is measureless, your mercy manifest.

PSALM 7: MY LORD, MY GOD, MY SONG OF PRAISE

O Lord, my God, in you I hide, pursuers are on every side.
Deliver me—they hunt my soul, their anger fierce, relentless, whole.
If guilt or wrong lies in my hand, if evil in my heart I planned,
Let justice come, let judgment fall, and turn my back against the wall.

Chorus
O righteous Judge, your name I praise, your hand upholds me all my days.
To you, Most High, my thanks belong, my hope, my shield, my victory song.

Arise, O Lord, and intervene, and let no evil come between.
Your justice reigns, your truth will test the hearts of all in righteousness.
The wicked fall in pits they make, their lies return, their scheming breaks.
Yet you, O Lord, my shield will be, your mercy guards and sets me free.

Chorus

Your sword is drawn, your bow is tight, to crush the wrong, defend the right.
The righteous stand, their hope secure, in you, O God, their hearts are pure.

Chorus and Outro
To you, Most High, my thanks I raise, my Lord, my God, my song of praise.

PSALM 8: O LORD, HOW GREAT IN MAJESTY

Chorus
O Lord, how great in majesty your name in all the earth!
Above the heavens your glory shines, proclaims your boundless worth.

When I behold the works you've made, the moon and stars set in their place,
    I marvel at your boundless power, your mercy, and your endless grace.
Who are we that you take note of us frail creatures formed from clay?
    And yet with glory you have crowned and honored us in every way.

Chorus

You've made us rulers of your works, all things beneath our feet,
    the beasts, the birds, the fish of seas—your sovereignty complete.
Through infants' praise and children's song, you silence every foe;
    your strength displayed in simple faith, your mighty works made known.

Chorus

Bridge
Forever may your name be praised, from age to endless age,
    for all creation lifts its voice, proclaiming you are great!
Let heaven and earth together sing with one harmonious chord:
    O Lord, our Lord, majestic is your name forevermore!

Chorus

PSALM 9: HOLY AND MIGHTY

Chorus
Holy and mighty, you reign above, righteous and merciful, filled with love.
Just and good your truth remains, forever, Lord, you do not change.

I thank you, Lord, with all my heart, your wondrous deeds set you apart.
I will be glad, exult in you, for who you are and what you do.

Chorus

I tell of all the works you've done, your justice and your victories won.
You lift me up from gates of death, so, I sing praise with every breath.

Chorus

You judge the world in righteousness, defending those who are oppressed.
A refuge strong for those in need, forsaking none whom you have freed.

Chorus

Bridge
Arise, O Lord, let nations see, your power and your sovereignty.
Confront them with mortality and in your mercy set them free.

The needy and poor remain in your heart, they are not forgotten, you set them apart,
For you are their refuge, their trust, and their shield, you will not forsake them; you hear their appeal.

Chorus

PSALM 10: ARISE, O LORD, AND HEAR THE CRY

Chorus
Hear, O Lord, the prayer of the grieved, strengthen their heart, in you they believe. Defending the orphan, the broken you save, no more let tyrants with terror enslave.

Why do the wicked boast in their pride? Why do they scorn and push you aside?
For in their hearts they think you forget, they seize the helpless without regret.

Chorus

You are the hope for the crushed and the poor, you see and provide them a refuge secure.
When darkness prevails your light overcomes, the humble you lift, the wicked succumbs.

Bridge
Arise, O Lord, lift up your hand, stand up for the broken throughout the land.
The afflicted commit their cause to you, you see, you hear, their foes subdue.

Chorus

Nations may tremble, empires may fall, but you reign eternal, the true Judge of all.
Your justice prevails, the wicked shall flee, your kingdom will triumph in victory!

Chorus and Outro
Arise, O Lord, and hear the cry, be near to the lowly, O God Most High!

PSALM 11: TRUTH AND JUSTICE SHALL PREVAIL

Flee, they cry, the night is falling, pointless now to take a stand.
Foundations gone, all is appalling, chaos sweeps across the land.
And yet my heart will not be shaken, God is just, of this I'm sure.
Though the wicked rise and threaten, still his purpose will endure.

Chorus
From his throne the Lord is reigning, watching both the strong and frail.
He is Judge of all the nations, truth and justice shall prevail.

Trials come to test and strengthen; faith's refined like precious gold.
Though the winds of doubt assail us, his promise and his truth will hold.
Blessed the one whose heart is steadfast, bearing every storm they face.
Crowned with life when trials are ended, kept by God's redeeming grace.

Chorus

Sin and death once held dominion, but the cross has set us free.
Christ has triumphed! Hell is vanquished! Now we stand in victory.
Hope compels us, love sustains us, faith will never turn aside.
The work of Jesus is completed, and so we stand against the tide.

Chorus

God will test, but not forsake us, his fire refines yet does not burn.
He plunges us into the struggle, yet his triumph we discern.
Stand, my soul, though trials gather, wait upon his sure decree.
In his time the proud will perish, and the righteous shall be free!

Chorus

Also based on James 1:2-4, 12; Colossians 2:13-15.

PSALM 12: TRUST IN GOD'S WORD

O Lord, we stand in darker days, surrounded by the proud,
Who, in deluded ignorance, boast and lie aloud.
They claim no master, bow to none, their words are false and vain,
But your words, Lord, are pure and true and over all you reign.

Chorus
Your words are pure, like silver bright, refined through flame, forever light.
The lies of all shall fade and fail, your truth divine shall yet prevail.

The groanings of the marginalized, the plundering of the weak.
You see their grief, you hear their cries, arise, dear Lord, and speak.
As once you heard the groans of slaves, so hear now once again,
Help those who cannot help themselves, and free them from their chains.

Chorus

On every side the wicked prowl, and vileness swells with pride.
You keep us safe, you keep us sure; you guard us from their lies.
As you have triumphed in the past, so show us once again,
That all who trust in you, O Lord, will not be put to shame.

Chorus

We are not masters of our way; our lives are yours alone.
A people called to trust and serve, to make your greatness known.
Surrounded by self-centeredness, we choose dependency
Upon your word, your character, your awesome sovereignty.

Chorus

Also based on Exodus 2:23–25; 6:5; Romans 3:4; Hebrews 6:18; 1 Peter 1:24–25.

PSALM 13: HOW LONG, O LORD?

How long, O Lord, will you forget, and hide your face away?
My heart is torn with deep regret, I strain for light of day.
My foe rejoices in my fall, my soul is filled with grief,
Yet still I lift my weary call: come swiftly, send relief!

Chorus
I trust your love, O Lord of light, your mercies never cease.
I will not fear through darkest night; in you I sleep in peace.

Upon the cross, 'gainst darkened sky, our Savior hung alone.
"Have you forsaken me?" he cried, words meant for those below.
'Cause in his death, new life was formed, our ransom fully paid,
In him creation is reborn, his glory to display.

Chorus

Through trials deep, my strength may fail, yet hope will not depart.
For though I may be weak and frail, God lifts my fainting heart.
O weary soul, press on in grace, though suff'ring may increase,
For Jesus walked this painful place, and bids all striving cease.

Chorus

"How long, O Lord?" your saints still plead, "How long before you save?"
Yet, though we wait, our hearts are freed in Jesus, strong and brave.
Our voices rise in endless praise, though struggles yet remain,
For crowned with glory, Lord, you raise us up with you to reign.

Chorus

Also based on Matthew 27:46; 2 Corinthians 1:8–9; Hebrews 12:3; Revelation 6:9–10.

PSALM 14: THE CROSS-SHAPED FOOLISHNESS OF GOD

The world denies, it turns away; ignoring God, from truth they hide.
"We choose," they say, "we base our lives on self-sufficiency and pride."
No heart seeks God, no one is pure, they chase their dreams and call them wise.
Forsaking wisdom, scorning grace, they blindly follow their own lies.

Chorus
But mercy shines, behold the cross! Where wisdom stands in love outpoured.
For though we fail through brokenness, we are forgiven through our Lord.
No heart could seek, no soul could rise yet love came down to set us free.
The cross-shaped foolishness of God demonstrates his love for me!

God looked for one who sought his face, but none were found, no righteous soul.
No human strength could bring us hope, yet still his mercy made us whole.
For love was sent in human frame, the Holy One for us was slain.
Despised, rejected by the wise, yet through his wounds we live again.

Chorus

So, lay your doubts and fears aside, come, bow before the risen Lord.
The message of the cross is power, it demonstrates God's final word.
The world may mock, the proud resist, in sinfulness remain enslaved.
The cross reveals what wisdom hides, God's grace is stronger than the grave!

Chorus

Also based on Isaiah 63:5; Romans 3:10–18; 5:8; 1 Corinthians 1:24–27; 1 John 4:9.

PSALM 15: HIS KINGDOM IS UNSHAKABLE

Who, O Lord, may dwell with you, those who do what's right and true?
Guiltless hands and hearts made pure, speaking truth that shall endure?
Yet none can claim a blameless way, because of sin we've gone astray.
Your law is right, your ways are good, but none have lived the way they should.

Chorus
Through Jesus, our identity has been renewed, we are set free.
Our names engraved upon his hands and held secure by his command.
No fear remains, we will not fall, his kingdom is unshakable!

Our sin had blocked the way to you, the world was torn, creation bruised.
But Jesus came, the Word made flesh, defeating Satan, sin, and death.
He tore the veil, he cleared the way, and called us out of night to day.
Now in his grace, we rise restored, with mercy rich and love outpoured.

Chorus

But now, no longer of the night, we live as citizens of light,
No fading hope, no fleeting prize, but minds renewed, transformed we rise.
Our lives reflect his truth and grace, his love at work in time and space.
We walk in justice, seek the good, and love as only Jesus could.

Chorus

Also based on Romans 3:23; 12:1–2; Ephesians 2:6–9; Hebrews 9:11–12, 24; 10:19–20; 12:22–24.

PSALM 16: I BLESS THE LORD WHO GUIDES MY WAY

Preserve me, O my God, I cry, for in your hands my refuge lies.
You are my Lord, my highest good, and I will follow as I should.

Chorus
I bless the Lord who guides my way, his wisdom leads me night and day.
I set my eyes on him alone, I am secure I am his own.

O God, my refuge, strong and sure, you hold me fast, I shall endure.
I have a safe inheritance in you my Lord, my confidence.

Chorus

My heart rejoices, I am glad, for Jesus rose up from the grave,
And his same Spirit lives in me, eternal life my destiny.

Chorus

You make me know the path of life; you walk with me through bitter strife,
With mercy guiding where I go; your presence brings unending joy.

Chorus

Also based on Acts 2:25–28; 13:35; Romans 8:11.

PSALM 17: I WILL RISE

Intro
Yes, I will rise, I will rise, in your likeness, in your light.
I will see you, face-to-face, satisfied I'll end my race.

When in my need I cry to you, Lord, hear my honest prayers.
You tried my heart, you found me true; please, save me from despair.
Reveal to me your steadfast love, O Savior of the meek.
Beneath the shadow of your wings save and keep the weak.

Chorus
But as for me, I shall behold your face in righteousness;
When you appear, we will be changed, forever we'll be blessed.
And I will wake in glory bright, like Jesus I will be!
For I shall see him as he is, my gracious God and King.

Because we share in flesh and blood, he likewise shared the same;
That through his death he might destroy the powers that ruled the grave.
He was rejected and betrayed, tried and put to death in hate,
Yet by his blood our debt was paid, their schemes undone, his victory great.

Chorus

The wicked rise on every side, their hearts are full of pride.
They seek to harm, they lay their snares, but you are by my side.
O Lord, arise, stretch out your hand, confront them and subdue.
Though darkness falls, you lift me up, your mercy shining through.

Chorus

My weary frame will fade to dust, yet in your hand remains
My hope, my confidence and trust; I will not be ashamed.

For as you live, so I will rise, transformed in love and changed.
And in your likeness satisfied, life for death exchanged.

Bridge
No more fading, no more crying, raised immortal, never dying!
Like the Son, we shine in splendor, in his presence, now and ever!
Chains are shattered, death defeated, Christ has won, the grave is beaten!

Chorus and Outro
Yes, I will rise, I will rise, in your likeness, in your light.
I will see you, face-to-face, satisfied I'll end my race.

Also based on 1 Corinthians 15:42–49; Colossians 2:14–15; Hebrews 2:14–15; 1 John 3:2; Revelation 22:4.

PSALM 18: OUR MIGHTY LORD

Chorus
I love you, Lord, you are my strength, my rock and my deliverer,
Redeemer, refuge, and my shield, my Savior and my comforter.

While darkness deep surrounded me, distress and fear my company.
I cried to you, I was afraid, I called on you, my God, for aid.
You heard my cry, you shook the ground, the mountains trembled at the sound.
The darkness fled before your light, you rode the storm and won the fight!

Chorus

From heaven, you have lifted me and saved me from calamity.
You brought me out and made me stand and you support me with your hand.
You lead me forth, my way is bright, for, Lord, you are my soul's delight.
With strength you arm my hands for war, my victory rests in you, O Lord!

Chorus

Bridge
Who is God except the Lord, the one who thunders and who roars?
A mighty God, and strong to save, who rules the wind and calms the waves.

Chorus and Outro
The Lord is strong, his love remains, forevermore I'll sing his praise!

PSALM 19: YOUR LOVE HAS CAPTURED ME

Creation shows your glory, Lord, the skies your handiwork.
Day to day revealing you, seen throughout the world.

Pre-Chorus
No speech, no words, and yet they cry, a melody of grace.
The stars above, the earth below, declare our Maker's face.
Chorus
Your love, the voice that calls my name, the light that leads me home.
Your word, the lamp that guides my way, the truth that makes me whole.
You made and you remake me Lord, your law has set me free,
For love's the law that rules the world, and that has captured me.

Your word revives the weary soul, it makes the simple wise.
Your rules are right and pure as gold, they open blinded eyes.

Pre-Chorus
You warn, you lead, you call us near to walk the path of life.
And in your truth we find our joy, your love is our delight.
Chorus

Who can discern their errors, Lord? We need your guiding hand.
Keep us from all presumptuous sins that blameless may we stand.

Bridge
Not by my strength, not by my will, but by your word alone.
For man shall live by every breath proceeding from your throne.

Pre-Chorus
And love came down to bear our shame, the weight of all our sin.
The cross reveals the heart of God, embracing us within.

Chorus and Outro
Let my words, my heart's desire, be pleasing in your sight.
My rock, my King, my righteousness, my joy, my love, my life.

PSALM 20: ONLY ONE ALMIGHTY REIGNS

When in distress I find myself, I turn to you in prayer.
My finite mind can't comprehend that you are everywhere.
But when I choose to look away from this apparent mess,
Beyond the cross, where hope seemed lost, the grave was dispossessed.

Chorus
Because I know the Lord has saved his chosen from the grave.
I am convinced that he will do the same for me and you.
So, do not trust in temporal might, but in the one who won the fight!
While many may collapse and fall, our Lord upholds us one and all.

When troubles cloud my vision, Lord, protect me from despair!
Remind me of your faithfulness, your never-changing care.
My steadfast hope and confidence is anchored in the past,
For though you suffered, though you died, God raised you up at last.

Chorus

Bridge
We know too well, from time to time, that flowers fade without sunshine.
You warn us in your holy word that hearts will break when hope's deferred.
Yet in despair the truth remains: that only one Almighty reigns.

Chorus

So, Father, grant my heart's desire as you fulfill your plans.
For just as Jesus's prayers were heard, you hear your precious lambs.
So, I will stand though trials come; you saved, you'll save again.
For as with Jesus, I will be, my cries are not in vain.

Chorus and Outro
Yes, in despair the truth remains: that only one Almighty reigns.

PSALM 21: I TRUST IN YOU, MY KING, MY LORD

In your salvation I exult, in you, Lord, I rejoice,
You gave to me my heart's desire, responding to my voice.
You set a crown upon my head of blessings rich and vast.
I asked and you have given me a future firm and fast.

Chorus
I trust in you, my King, my Lord, and through your steadfast love
I stand secure, immoveable, with blessings from above.
My trust is in your mighty name, my victory is sure,
And you will place upon my brow a crown that will endure.

You've raised me to your throne above, I'm seated with my Lord.
And through your loving purposes I press on toward the goal.
And though the fight is fierce and long, my feet will never stray.
The power of your outstretched arm will guide me all the way.

Chorus

Bridge
Run the race! Lift your eyes! Set your gaze upon the prize.
By his power we endure, for his mercy keeps us pure.
He has triumphed! He has won! All his foes will be undone.
Glory, honor, all renown, to the King who wears the crown!

O Lord, you reign in righteousness, your justice fills the land.
Your enemies will fall in fear, before your mighty hand.
Despite my failure and my falls, I rise and run the race.
For Jesus conquered death and sin and saved me by his grace!

Chorus and Outro
So, we run, upheld by grace, till we see you face-to-face!

Also based on 1 Corinthians 9:24–27; 15:25; Ephesians 2:4–10.

PSALM 22: FROM DARKNESS TO GLORY

O God, my God, why hide your face, why seem so far in my distress?
Yet, in your mercy and your grace, I am compelled to reassess.
Our fathers called; you heard their plea, delivered them from slavery.

Chorus
From darkness deep your light has shone, your love through sacrifice is shown.
Through cross and grave, the victory won, all glory be to Christ alone!

Despised, rejected, scorned with shame, those all around me seek my hurt.
Yet in my pain, I praise your name, for you, O Lord, do not desert.
Not far from me my Savior stays, redeems me through his chosen ways.

Chorus

The nations now shall hear your voice, the grieved shall feast within your halls.
The ends of earth in you rejoice, your kingdom reigns above them all.
All knees shall bow, all tongues confess, the Lord of life brings righteousness.

Chorus

Let generations yet unborn proclaim the wonders you have done.
For Christ has borne our grief and scorn and triumphed as the risen Son.
Your name forever we shall raise, in endless songs of holy praise.

Chorus and Outro
All glory be to Christ alone, Redeemer, Savior, on the throne!

PSALM 23: MY SHEPHERD KING

The Lord's my Shepherd, I'll not fear, for he is with me, he is near.
He knows my need before I pray, his mercy meets me every day.
The sparrows sing, the flowers bloom, he fills the earth with sweet perfume.
Why should I strive, why should I hoard? He is enough, I need no more.

He calls my name; I hear his voice. He leads me by his sovereign choice.
By quiet streams and pastures wide he makes a home where I reside.
He walks ahead, his path is sure, 'cause he's the way and he's the door,
Through him alone my steps are safe, he leads me onward to his place.

When I am down I will recall that he restores me when I fall.
For righteousness he leads me on, till all that's dark in me is gone.
For as I walk he will repair, with his amazing, loving care,
The things in me that are not right, till I reflect his glorious light.

Chorus
But greater still is that my Lord is with me in the darkest gorge,
I need not fear for he defends, lays down his life for me, his friend.
He takes me from my dungeoned night to place me in his realm of light,
For in the darkness at the cross, my life was found that once was lost.
He bore my sin, he crushed the grave, his blood is powerful to save.
No fear, no foe, no power remains; my Shepherd King's the one who reigns!

A feast is laid, a table set, in stark relief against each threat.
My Shepherd acts as gracious host, providing to the uttermost.
But more than host—the Bread of Life becomes the final sacrifice!
Prepares a table and a place for us to live before his face.

And now may my great God of peace, who, for the sake of his own sheep,
Raised up our Shepherd from the dead to save us from the things we dread,

Lead us on in endless grace, until we see him face-to-face.
So, we will live, redeemed and free, in endless light and victory.

Bridge
The banquet set, the call goes wide; the Groom has come to claim his Bride!
O blessed eucharistic feast; our Shepherd is our great High Priest.

Chorus and Outro
The banquet set, the call goes wide; the Groom has come to claim his Bride!
O blessed eucharistic feast; our Shepherd is our great High Priest.

Also based on Matthew 6:25–34; 28:20; Mark 7:7–11; 15:25; Luke 22:15–20; John 6:35, 51–56; 10:3–4, 9, 11–18; 14:2, 6; 1 Corinthians 5:7; Ephesians 2:10; Colossians 1:12–14; Titus 2:14; Hebrews 9:14; 13:10–12, 20–21; Revelation 19:9.

PSALM 24: THE KING OF GLORY REIGNS

The earth is doubly yours, O Lord, for by your word it stands,
Yet you have bought it with your life, the work of nail-pierced hands.
The sea, the land, the sky, and all—each one is yours by right,
For all who live and breathe on earth belong within your light.

And yet, through sin, the way to you is barred and guarded well.
Who may ascend to come before you as all have rebelled?
Only those whose hearts are pure, whose hands have not done wrong,
Whose souls have not been compromised, in whom no fraud is found.

Chorus
Lift up your heads, and open wide, you ancient gates and doors.
The one who knew no sin is here, withdraw and stand in awe.
The King of Glory rides in might, no power can withstand,
The sovereign reign of Jesus Christ, all bow to his command.

In every way he was like us and yet he knew no sin,
By death he has defeated death, and he has entered in.
Ascending to his throne on high, our Lord sat down to reign,
And now all people must resolve to bow before the King!

The universe belongs to him who sits upon the throne,
Yet with our eyes we may not see all serving him alone.
And yet the gates will not prevail against his strong advance,
As Jesus leads his Church along to plunder hell's expanse.

Chorus

Bridge
Now bow before his mighty name, and with your tongues confess
That Jesus Christ is Lord of all, the King of Glory blessed.

Chorus and Outro
Both heaven's heights and hell's despair
Must yield before the King declared!

Also based on Daniel 7:13–14; Matthew 5:8; 28:18; John 1:3; Acts 1:9–11; 3:21; 1 Corinthians 10:26; 15:24–28; Philippians 2:10–11; Colossians 1:16–17; 2:14–15; Hebrews 2:8–9; 10:19–22; 12:22–24; James 4:8; Revelation 19:11–16.

PSALM 25: TEACH ME YOUR WAYS

My soul I lift to you, my Lord, my God in whom I trust;
Let me be never put to shame, O Savior of the just.
Through storm and trial, I won't be moved, I know whom I've believed;
I am convinced that he will guard and keep what I've received.

Chorus
So, make me know your ways, O Lord, and lead me in your truth.
Save me from presumptuous sins, transgressions from my youth.
In steadfast love remember me, for you are good and right.
Your faithfulness, your mercy, Lord, will lead me to your light.

Instruct and show me by your grace the road that leads to life;
When I am lonely, when I'm lost, when overwhelmed with strife,
Consider my afflicted soul and free me from the net.
Turn to me in graciousness, O Lord, do not forget.

Chorus

Bridge
Redeem me from my troubles, Lord, for I consider loss,
The many things I once held dear and nailed them to the cross!

Chorus

No longer will I be estranged; no longer will I cringe.
You call me friend, you call me near to you my gracious King.
No longer shall my enemy exult over my faults.
Your perfect love has cast out fear and silenced his assaults.

Chorus and Outro
Preserve me in your uprightness, O Lord, I wait on you.

Also based on John 15:15; Philippians 3:8–10; Colossians 2:14; 2 Timothy 1:12.

PSALM 26: ON SOLID GROUND

When darkness comes, where can I turn to plead my innocence
If those who should uphold the law abandon righteousness?
Yet I have walked in faithfulness and in integrity,
So, search me, test me, shine your light, O Lord, please answer me.

Chorus
But as I lift my eyes to you to gaze upon the cross,
I find perspective and my peace in you who save the lost.
Washed in the fountain of your grace, I see my sins erased.
The accuser's voice is silenced now, with Jesus I am raised.

I have not sat with those who lie, with those whose lives are false,
Who fabricate a piety to use in their assault.
The innocent become their prey; they seek to justify
Their wicked schemes against the just; their hands are full of bribes.

Chorus

In anguish in Gethsemane you prayed and cried aloud,
Your tears fell heavy in the night; you heard the coming crowd.
Yet in surrender you obeyed, enduring their disdain
For you had set your mind upon the one who vindicates.

Bridge
When no one hears my God still sees, through every trial he hears my pleas,
With no recourse his truth remains, his faithfulness my hope sustains!

Chorus and Outro
On solid ground, my feet are firm, and openly I will confirm
That God is just and good and true, in Jesus I have been renewed.

Also based on Luke 22:40–47; Hebrews 5:7–9.

PSALM 27: MY ONE REQUEST

Lord, you are my true salvation, I will not be frightened.
You're my safe and only refuge; in you I am enlightened.
Even though I am encircled, troubles that surround me,
I believe, of this I'm certain, you are always with me.

Chorus
I have only one enquiry; I have only one request:
That I may gaze, all of my days, upon your beauty blessed.
Forgetting all that lies behind me and pressing on to gain the prize:
That upward call, gifted to all, who are in Jesus Christ.

Hear, O Lord, my one petition, graciously indulge me.
Seeking you, my only passion, please do not forsake me.
Even those meant to be gentle, they may fall and scatter.
You have been my help and shelter; you are all that matters.

Chorus

Bridge
Lift me high upon the rock; keep me safely in your flock.
No more crying, no more tears; no more lost and wasted years.

Chorus

Also based on Philippians 3:13–14.

PSALM 28: O FATHER GOD, YOU ARE OUR ROCK

O Father God, you are our rock, we lift our prayers to you
For you alone are God on high, please hear us when we call.

Pre-Chorus
You are our strength, you are our shield, our stronghold safe and fortress sealed.
Chorus
O Father, let your kingdom come, and let your will be done
On earth just as it is in heaven, until we've overcome.
Be our Shepherd, grant our needs, forgive our doubts, help us believe.

Dear Father, in your clemency, hear us as we grieve.
Don't let our hearts be drawn to pride, forgive as we forgive.

Pre-Chorus and Chorus

Bridge
Deliver us from all that's wrong, you hold the power, you are strong.
Forever faithful, just, and true, kingdom glory belongs to you.

Pre-Chorus, Chorus, and Outro
You are our strength, you are our shield, our stronghold safe and fortress sealed.

Also based on The Lord's Prayer

PSALM 29: CRY GLORY!

Before all things, the Word was spoken, light and life began to shine.
God Almighty rules eternal, inexpressibly sublime.

Pre-Chorus
Worthy! You are worthy! For by you all things were created,
By you all things are sustained, you alone are in control.
Chorus
Glory! We cry glory! To the one who rules the waters,
To the one who shakes the earth. Glory! We cry glory!
Acknowledge him your only Master, worship Christ your only King.

Thunder roars, the cedars shatter, at his word the storms obey.
Yet his whisper lifts the weary, bids the fawn see light of day.

Pre-Chorus and Chorus

Bridge
His voice can break the strongest tree; his voice can set the prisoner free;
His voice like thunder speaks his word and yet in stillness he is heard.

Christ, the Power of creation, Christ, the one who re-creates.
Every power and foundation bow the knee to celebrate!

Pre-Chorus, Chorus, and Outro
The Lord enthroned, our strength, our peace, his reign eternal will not cease.

Also based on Genesis 1:1–3; 1 Kings 19:11–12; Philippians 2:9–11; Colossians 1:15–20.

PSALM 30: WE WILL EXTOL YOU

To you, O Lord, we cry aloud; O God do not desert us!
What gain is there if we're destroyed and cast into the abyss?
True, there is not one of us whom Satan has not broken.
Although we try, we always fail; from death we must be woken.

Pre-Chorus
We are undone; we are condemned. Who will save us? Who'll defend?
Chorus
We will extol you, O our Lord, for you have drawn us up
From hell and from destruction, from all that is corrupt.
Through death you have defeated death, in resurrection conquered.
Thanks be to God who, through our Lord, the sting of death defeated.

And so, in our calamity, when weeping through the night,
We look and we consider him, who won for us the fight.
For even though he feared the cross, for joy he persevered,
Despised the shame, and earned the name above all names revered.

Pre-Chorus
We are renewed; we are forgiven. In our Lord we'll not be shaken.
Chorus

Bridge
You turned our mourning into dancing, our sadness you have clothed with joy.
Our hearts will sing and not be silent, in you the grave has been destroyed.

Chorus and Outro
Thanks be to God who, through our Lord, the sting of death defeated.

Also based on Romans 7; 1 Corinthians 15; Hebrews 12.

PSALM 31: INTO YOUR HANDS

Verse 1 (John's perspective)
I stand beneath the darkening sky, the weight of sorrow in my chest,
The one who calmed the raging sea now wracked in pain with every breath.
Dear God, shall we be put to shame by those who schemed against our Lord?
Their lying lips have won the day, they crucified your living Word.

Pre-Chorus
O my Lord, my dearest Friend, is this now how our story ends?
Chorus
But no, we hear your rasping voice cry, "Father, in your hand
I do commit my living soul." And so, our hearts demand
That we recall the psalm in which those very words were said,
A psalm that speaks of love and trust and triumph over dread.
And though the grave may take your breath, in suffering there is hope.

Verse 2 (Mary's perspective)
I held his hands when he was small, and Joseph taught him how to build.
We watched him blossom as he grew and saw the prophecies fulfilled.
But now he bleeds upon this tree, and there is nothing I can do.
Is he forgotten as the dead? My heart is pierced and cut in two.

Pre-Chorus
O my son, my precious one, is this now how victory's won?
Chorus

Bridge
Be strong, take heart O weary ones, the night will end, the dawn will come.
Though death may strike it won't prevail, grace and mercy will not fail.

Verse 3 (Peter's perspective)

Be gracious to me, O my God, for I am in distress.
My eyes are dry from dreadful grief, my mind is not at rest.
For, in my fear, I shunned my Lord, denied the one I loved.
What is my life but sorrow now? My future has been crushed.

Pre-Chorus
O my Lord, how can there be clemency for one like me?
Chorus

Outro
Into your hands he placed his soul and death was crushed and lost control.
The grave is empty, hope remains, Christ is on the throne to reign.

PSALM 32: BLESSED ARE THE FORGIVEN

Chorus
I will not hide, I will not run, though sin has rendered me undone.
Though nothing good is found in me, in your forgiveness I'm set free.
By my obedience to your word, I walk in trust though ways are blurred.
Your faithfulness, as I confess, will cleanse me from unrighteousness.

Blessed is the one whose sins are gone; their slate wiped clean by you alone.
No debt remains, no stain of pride, but by your grace they're justified.
But while my sins were unconfessed, my heart within me was depressed.
Both day and night I groaned inside, but then I prayed, and you replied.

Chorus

Instruct and teach me in your way, so that I may not go astray.
Give me counsel, keep me safe, protect me in your hiding place.

Bridge
Seek the Lord while he is near, call his name, for he will hear.
True and just, he heeds my plea, lifts my weight, and covers me.
Surrounds me with his endless love, his grace and mercy are enough.

Chorus and Outro
Your faithfulness, as I confess, will cleanse me from unrighteousness.

Also based on Isaiah 55:6; Romans 4:6–8; 1 John 1:9; 1 Peter 3:12.

PSALM 33: THE LOVE THAT FILLS THE EARTH

Intro
Shout for joy and lift your voice, for praise befits the righteous!
Give thanks to God for he is good, as he loves truth and justice.

Not by strength of governments, not by the knowledge learned,
Not by our ingenuity is future life confirmed.
But by a love that does not cease, a voice that speaks what's true,
And by the hand that shaped it all and carries me and you.

Chorus
The steadfast love that fills the earth, the power that does not fade,
The thread that binds the universe, the breath that calls our names.
We rise, we fall, we vanish, but love and truth remain,
The steadfast love that fills the earth still governs and restrains.

The nations trust in weapons, the greedy seek for gold,
In error they seek wisdom and call the reckless bold.
God brings their plans to nothing; his justice does not sleep.
The proud will fade like embers, the wicked rise and weep.

Bridge
The love that made the galaxies still whispers in the dark;
He watches over everyone and stills our anxious hearts.

Chorus and Outro
Shout for joy and lift your voice, for praise befits the righteous!
Give thanks to God for he is good, as he loves truth and justice.

PSALM 34: TASTE AND SEE!

Come, O saints, and lift your voices, magnify the Lord with me.
Though our hearts be bruised and broken, we should praise him constantly.
Despite my fears, despite my weakness, God is watching over me.
Now my lips proclaim his goodness, come, O taste and you will see!

Chorus
Taste and see! The Lord is with us, at his table, grace abounds.
Here is life born from affliction, here the Crucified is found.

Angel hosts encamp around us, guarding those who trust his name.
Though the night is filled with weeping, still his love remains the same.
Come, you weary, come, you hungry, come, you lost in dark despair.
At his feast, the cup of mercy waits for all who gather there.

Chorus

Many trials press in upon us, yet the Lord will bring us through.
Not one sorrow, not one burden, lies beyond what he can do.
He is near the crushed in spirit, he upholds the faint, the poor.
See, the wounds that bought redemption; by his death we are secure.

Chorus

Bridge
O the Lamb of God has suffered, O the Lamb of God has bled.
Yet from sorrow springs salvation, from his cross—the feast of bread!

Chorus

PSALM 35: YOU, O LORD, ARE KING OF ALL

O Lord, arise and plead my cause! Take up your shield, unsheathe your sword!
Against the proud, against their claims defend the ones who trust your Word.
Let those who hunt my life in hate be turned away and put to flight,
Let them be subject to their fate, their evil swallowed by the night.

They lay their snares, they forge their lies, they mock my grief, they scorn my tears.
I wept for them when sorrows rose, yet now they stab with taunts and jeers.
O God, how long will you delay? How long will justice sleep unseen?
Rise up, O Lord! Reveal yourself and make my strife fade like a dream.

Chorus
For you, O Lord, you see, you know! The wicked scheme, the righteous bleed,
But truth shall rise, and justice flow, divine defense for those in need.
Let all who love your holy name, rejoice to see your kingdom come,
For Satan's plots shall end in shame, and all the earth shall call you Lord!

Then I shall sing with pure delight, my tongue shall sing your boundless grace!
The orphaned heart shall dance in light, the poor shall see your glorious face.
O Lord, be near! O Lord, be strong! The weary wait in shattered trust.
Let mercy write our victor's song and crush the serpent in the dust.

Chorus
For you, O Lord, you see, you reign! In you your children are secure.
Though trials come, though foes disdain, your steadfast love shall still endure.
Let every voice confess your name, let nations totter, empires fall!
The righteous Judge has won his claim, and you, O Lord, are King of all!

Outro
Let every voice confess your name, let nations totter, empires fall!
The righteous Judge has won his claim, and you, O Lord, are King of all!

PSALM 36: THE STEADFAST LOVE OF GOD

Your steadfast love, O Lord, is boundless, beyond the furthest galaxy.
Your righteousness like mighty mountains, your faithfulness past all we see.
Your judgments deeper than the oceans, in your presence, we're secure.
Feasting on your great abundance, drinking from your river pure.

Pre-Chorus
From you the spring of life pours out, and in your light do we see light.
Chorus
Hallelujah! Love unmeasured, God Almighty, strong to save!
Who can stand against his mercy? Who can steal what Jesus gave?
Depth and height cannot divide us, it is God who justifies;
Not one thing in all creation moves the ones for whom he died.

Your steadfast love, O Lord, is proven, verified through Christ who died.
In Jesus love is demonstrated, measured by the Crucified.
Laying down his life for sinners, wiping out required debt,
Eliminating condemnation, charges against the Lord's elect.

Pre-Chorus and Chorus

Spirit, strengthen us with power, root and ground us, help us see
Love that passes understanding binds us all inseparably.
Breadth and length and height unmeasured, depths no mind could yet explore,
Filling us with all your fullness, dwell in us forevermore.

Pre-Chorus and Chorus

Doxology:
Now to him whose power is working, far beyond what we conceive,
Be all glory and all honor to the one whom we believe.

Praise unceasing, never ending, to the King upon the throne,
Throughout every generation sing his name, and his alone!

Also based on Romans 8:31–39; Ephesians 3:16–12.

PSALM 37: GOD WILL UPHOLD THE RIGHTEOUS

Don't fret yourself, O weary one, when wickedness increases.
For what appears as strong today will soon fall into pieces.
Trust in the Lord and do his will, in all things remain faithful;
Make him the centre of your life and in your prayers be grateful.

When darkness seems to overwhelm and hopelessness seems greater,
Commit yourself to God alone and trust in your Creator.
In economic tragedy his children aren't forsaken;
He still provides and will prevail, so they may be a blessing.

Chorus
So, turn away from misery and redirect your focus!
God rules the world in majesty, in rightness, and in justice.
The timeless question still may be, Does Jesus even notice?
Be still, be patient, wait and see, God will uphold the righteous.

Though ruthless people plot and boast and threaten every portal,
A little while, they'll be no more, like every other mortal.
The Lord will not abandon us, for though we may yet stumble
We will not fall, for he upholds the honest and the humble.

The little that the righteous own is better than abundance,
For shame remains for those whose wealth was gathered without conscience.
God knows the days and shapes the ways of those whose lives are yielded,
And he delights in everyone whose hearts are not conceited.

So, mark the faithful, watch their way, for they will be delivered.
For though petitions seem delayed, God's promise will not linger.
For we are called as witnesses, for vivid illustrations
That faith and trust and godliness will overcome frustrations.

Chorus

PSALM 38: COME REST IN ME, YOU HEAVY-LADEN

O Lord, my soul is bowed in sorrow, the weight of sin too much to bear.
My strength is gone, my hope is fading, I need your mercy, meet me here.

Pre-Chorus
And in the dark, your voice is calling . . .
Chorus
Come, rest in me you heavy-laden, lay down your burdens at the cross.
Come learn from me for I am gentle, come walk with me and be refreshed.

I will confess my deep transgression, my sins have gone over my head.
I do not come with vain pretension, with empty hands I come instead.

Pre-Chorus
And even now, your arms are open . . .
Chorus

Forsaken, scorned, alone he suffered, the Sinless One bore all my shame.
And by his wounds my soul is ransomed, forgiven in his holy name.

Bridge
O the blood that speaks my pardon, O the grace that sets me free!
Jesus bore my sin and sorrow, now I live in liberty.

Pre-Chorus
Still now he speaks with love unshaken . . .
Chorus

Also based on Matthew 11:28–30; Luke 18:13; 1 John 1:9.

PSALM 39: MY HOPE IS SET ON YOU

O Lord, I stand in silence, too burdened now to speak.
My fleeting days are passing, a breath, a fading dream.
What riches shall I cling to? What kingdom shall I build?
All crumbles into nothing, yet still my hope is you.

Chorus
Teach me to number all my days, to see how brief they are.
A shadow, like the morning mist, a flower soon to fade.
Yet still I lift my cry to you: O Lord do not delay!

Like moths consume the fabric, so time wears down my years.
We rise, we shine, we wither and vanish in our tears.
Yet in this fleeting moment, my soul will rest secure.
I turn my eyes to heaven, the city that endures.

Chorus

Bridge
A stranger here, a pilgrim, I journey to my home.
By faith my heart has tasted the joy before your throne.
This world is not my dwelling, my treasure lies above.
O Lord, do not forget me, embrace me in your love.

Chorus

Also based on Hebrews 11.

PSALM 40: I WILL PROCLAIM

I waited on you, O my Lord, you heard my cry, you answered me
You raised me from the pit of ruin, you lifted and established me.
You put a new song in my mouth, a song of praise to you my God,
That many hearts may turn to you and put their trust in you, my Lord.

Chorus
O blessed are the ones who stand not in the pride of sinful man,
But in your strong, redeeming hand and live by your divine commands.
Your wondrous deeds you have increased, your gracious thoughts I do recall.
Not one on earth compares to you, I will proclaim and tell them all!

No sacrifice my hands could bring, no offering could cleanse my shame.
But in the Scriptures you foretold that one would come to take my blame.
"Behold, I come to do your will!" and on the cross he freely bore
The bonds of my captivity, no condemnation anymore!

Chorus

I speak of your deliverance, I will not hide your faithfulness,
I won't restrain my utterance, I tell of your trustworthiness.
For you, O Lord, have not restrained your steadfast love and graciousness,
Compassionate and merciful, unmatched in your attentiveness.

Bridge
May all who seek you with one voice sing praises to you and rejoice.
For you are great and powerful; to me, O Lord, you're wonderful!

Chorus

PSALM 40: I WILL NOT HIDE FROM ANYONE

My way was dark, my hope was gone, and yet he stooped to hear my cry.
He pulled me from the darkest pit to cleanse and freely justify.
He placed a new song in my mouth, a hymn of praise the world must hear.
For on the cross he conquered hell and now my way to life is clear.

Chorus
I will not hide from anyone what you have done through your own Son.
I won't conceal what you've revealed, Lord, speak through me, make your appeal!

Your wondrous deeds are staggering, your graciousness beyond compare,
Your thoughts for us are always good, you hear before we speak our prayers!
No sacrifice or offering could ever take away my sin,
But on the cross you demonstrate a love that cannot be hidden.

Bridge
Though poor and weak I shall not fear, for Jesus you are always near.
You lift me up, you hold my days, you send me out to sing your praise!

Chorus

You sent your Son, the Word made flesh, for nothing here could bring us life.
Through him we have our righteousness! Our one and final sacrifice.
Now send us forth, your word in hand, till every nation, tribe, and tongue
Has heard the truth in every land that through our Lord the battle's won.

Chorus

PSALM 41: WHO IS LIKE THE LORD OUR GOD?

Who lifts the stranded from the dust and helps those whom the world ignores?
Who sees the lowly, loves the lost, renews what has not been before?
The Lord, the Lord, our strong salvation, he'll not turn his face away!
He'll raise the poor and soothe the weary, the lowly he'll not lead astray!

Chorus
Who is like the Lord our God? Crowned, majestic, robed in light,
He once was dead yet now alive, ruling in tremendous might.
In him all things are reconciled, the new creation has begun.
Who is like the Lord our God? Worship him, the only one.

The hands that fed were struck and bound, the lips he trusted deceived and lied,
The Righteous One was left alone, denied, and tried, and crucified.
But God has raised him to his throne, no grave can hold the Lord of light!
The King betrayed, the Lamb afflicted, now sits enthroned in glorious might!

Chorus

The Lord is faithful, strong, and true, his kingdom stands, his word remains.
Though nations rage and kings conspire, his promises no one can change.
The humble feast at Jesus's table, the broken find their refuge there,
The Lord has spoken, none can hinder, let every heart in awe draw near!

Chorus

BOOK TWO

Psalms 42–72

PSALM 42: O MY SOUL, WHY ARE YOU WEARY?

As the deer in thirst is calling for the streams that quench and fill,
So, my soul, in anguish falling, longs to know my Savior's will.
Day and night my tears have spoken, Where is he, my hope, today?
Yet his love is still unbroken, still his mercy lights my way.

Chorus
O my soul, why are you weary? Why detained in doubt's embrace?
Hope in God, though night is dreary; shadow soon will be displaced!

I recall the songs of thunder, when our people sang with might;
Yet now as I sit and ponder, lost within my silent night,
Waves of sorrow, deep and endless, flood my heart and shake my trust.
Yet his promise stands unshaken: he is near, and he is just.

Chorus

Still, his steadfast love upholds me, still, his grace my victory song.
Though my mortal senses fail me, faith shall rise and make me strong!
I will trust in God, my Savior, through the storm and deep distress,
Till my doubts are stilled forever, and I've banished Satan's threats!

Final Chorus
O my soul, lift up your praises! Sing, for he will not forsake!
Hope in God, the rock unshaken, Christ is raised, my soul awake!

PSALM 43: HOPE IN GOD; FOR I SHALL AGAIN PRAISE HIM

In the shadows where I sorrow, where I languish in the dark,
God, my refuge, God, my stronghold, why so bleak and why so stark?

Pre-Chorus
Where is my God, the one I seek? Where is the lamp to light my feet?
How can I come when all I see are broken paths of treachery?
Chorus
O my God, send out your mercy, let your light and truth draw near!
Lift my soul from doubt and darkness, guide my steps and calm my fears.

Waves of anguish crash around me, every prayer seems lost at sea.
Yet I stand, though torn and broken, struck, but not in misery.

Pre-Chorus and Chorus

Bridge
Through my tears and through my breaking, through the silence and the strain,
Still your Word is ever speaking, still your promise will remain.

Now I see dawn's early splendor, hope will never put to shame.
Faith revives where once I stumbled, grace has turned my loss to gain.

Pre-Chorus
You have called me to your mountain, to the city of the free,
To the throne where saints and angels sing your praise eternally.
Final Chorus
O my God, send out your mercy, Let your light and truth draw near!
Lift my soul from doubt and darkness, Bring me home; my joy is here!

Also based on John 8:12; 14:6; Romans 5:3–5; 2 Corinthians 4:6–9; Hebrews 12:22–24.

PSALM 44: WHO CAN STAND AGAINST HIS OWN?

O my God, in adoration, we recall the days of old,
How your hand upheld and guided, how you raised the weak and bold.
Not by sword or strength of warriors, but by love you gave release,
You inspired our fleeting stories, you bequeathed us homes and peace.

Chorus
If our God is for his people, who shall stand against his own?
Neither trial nor tribulation, depth nor height, nor things unknown,
Neither death nor condemnation, nor the dark that veils the sky
Can remove us from his mercy; Christ has claimed, who can defy?

You alone, our King and Shepherd, still command our foes to flee.
Through your name we stand unshaken, never fearing enemies.
Now the night has closed upon us, wolves surround us, thieves destroy;
Vulnerable, exposed and helpless, where's the peace we once enjoyed?

Chorus

Yet, dear Lord, have you forgotten? Circumstances strike us low.
Where is now the hand that lifted, where the strength that crushed our foe?
We have held to truth unswerving; we have kept the laws you gave.
Yet we lie in dust, forsaken, as a victim in a grave.

Bridge 1
Yet Christ was bruised, yet Christ was broken, through wounds of love salvation sealed.
For love's great cause we stand forsaken, like slaughtered sheep upon the field.

Chorus

Shall the dark declare its triumph? Shall the silence mock our cries?
Will you, Lord, be still forever while the scoffer scorns our sighs?
Wake, O God! Rise up in mercy! For your love dispels the night.
By your promise come redeem us, clothe us once again in light!

Bridge 2
For these trials are light and fleeting, shadows cast before the dawn.
What we see will soon be swallowed, only what is true lives on.
Lift your eyes beyond the suffering, see the glory yet to come!

Chorus

Also based on Romans 8:31–39; 2 Corinthians 4:17–18.

PSALM 45: THE BRIDEGROOM AND HIS BRIDE

As I gaze upon your beauty as revealed within your Word,
Like a flood, I'm inundated and my heart is deeply stirred.
O my King, how bright your glory, clothed in splendor, crowned in grace!
Like a scribe, with flowing poetry I will praise you in this place.

Mighty One, ride forth in triumph for the cause of righteousness;
Truth and mercy are your standards, blazing with your graciousness.
With your Word dispel the darkness, cast down principalities,
Bring an end to all oppression, Satan's vile brutalities.

Chorus
Everlasting is your throne, O God, scepter firm in your right hand.
You have loved the ways of righteousness, sin withdrawn at your command.
With oil of joy, you are ascended, lifted up above the rest.
Waves of myrrh and perfumed spices flow; in your fragrance we're refreshed.

Daughter, rise in robes of radiance, garments wrought of woven light.
Leave behind the fading kingdom, come and be your King's delight.
Jewelled halls resound with music, gems of splendor gild the walls.
Nations turn to see the beauty of the Bride of Christ installed.

Sword upon your thigh, O Victor, ride in majesty and might!
Every foe shall fall before you, demons tremble at your sight.
King of kings, the dawn is breaking, may all nations know your name!
Bride and Bridegroom, one forever, shining like the brightest flame.

Chorus

Cause your name to be remembered, generations yet unborn.
Every knee shall bow before you, every voice declare you Lord.

Christ the King, your name exalted, highest throne forevermore!
Every crown of every kingdom laid before you on the floor.

Also based on Philippians 2:9–11; Revelation 19:11–16.

PSALM 46: LIFT YOUR EYES; BEHOLD HIS KINGDOM!

When the nations shake and crumble, when the earth dissolves in fear,
When the wars of men are raging, still the Lord of hosts is here.
Not in power, wealth, or wisdom, not in rulers set to fall,
But in Christ, the King eternal, God is reigning over all.

Chorus
There's a river, vast, unmeasured, flowing from the throne of God.
Through the Tree of Life he thunders, surging strong with life and love.
No more death and no more sorrow, former things have passed away.
There's no need of moon or sunlight, God's glory shines as bright as day.

See the Lamb in triumph seated, once was slain but now he reigns.
From his midst the Spirit flowing to cleanse the world of every stain.
Through the wasteland hope is stirring, deserts bloom where he has flowed.
Cleansing, healing, and convicting, every curse to overthrow.

Chorus

Kingdoms rise and fall in ashes, nations boast then fade away.
Still his voice resounds in thunder, powers flee and are dismayed.
Structures of the universe break down and fall apart,
But God is stable and eternal, he's the Lord of every heart.

Chorus

So, stop and think! Evaluate. Temporal hopes will not endure.
Shifting empires, fading riches, only God is strong and sure!
Lift your eyes; behold his kingdom! Turn and tremble, stand in awe!
Seek him now, your one salvation! Come and serve him, Lord of all.

Also based on John 7:37–39; Ezekiel 47:1–12; Revelation 21:2–7; 22:1–5.

PSALM 47: THE KING ENTHRONED

In clouds of glory he ascended, blasts of trumpet pageantry.
To him was given all dominion, in heaven and earth authority.
Tens of thousands in his presence, angels and archangels too,
The Lamb once slain now reigns eternal, grave and death he overthrew.

Chorus
Lift up your voices, people sing! Great and awesome is our King!
He rules the earth, upholds the spheres, and he will reign for endless years.

He breaks the pride of mighty heads and gathers those the world derides.
No throne endures except his own, no name but his will fill the skies.
All peoples live beneath his rule, he will advance though sins increase.
The Lord alone remains supreme, his aim to bring in endless peace.

Chorus

The mountains bow, the rivers dance, the trees rejoice, their hands are raised.
The songs of saints and angels swell in hallowed worship and in praise.
The Lord who rules in holiness has claimed his own and set them free.
Let every nation with one voice acclaim the King's great victory.

Chorus
Hallelujah! Christ ascended, reigning as our conquering King.
The marriage of the Lamb has come, let the Bride his praises sing!

Behold, he comes! The skies are torn, the trumpet sounds as he descends.
The one whose name is just and true will bring all powers to an end.
Then at his coming all will see the one they pierced, the one they bruised.
His enemies beneath his feet. All in subjection to his rule.

Chorus
Hallelujah! Christ descending; do not grieve for those who died.
All are raised to live forever, in him all are glorified.

Worthy is the Lamb ascended!
Worthy is our righteous King!
Worthy he who must be honored!
Worthy! Worship! We will sing!

Also based on Psalm 110:1; Isaiah 55:12; Daniel 7:14; Zechariah 14:91; Matthew 28:18–20; Acts 1:8; 1 Corinthians 15:25–27; Ephesians 4:8; 1 Thessalonians 4:16; Revelation 1:7; 15:3–4; 19:6–8, 11–16.

PSALM 48: THE NEW JERUSALEM

Great is the Lord, great to be praised, forever constant, he'll not change.
His throne is stable and secure, his justice holy, bright, and pure.
Opponents tremble at his sight, they will panic and retreat,
Overwhelmed and put to flight by one whose victory is complete.

Chorus
Behold the city, come and see the throne of God in majesty;
The Lamb is seated by his side, his river flowing deep and wide.
No more day and no more night, the Lord our God will be our light.

Within his courts resounds the praise of saints who stand with hands upraised.
Among his people he resides; no temple there, for God abides.
No shadow falls, no death is near, no evil dares to enter in.
No death, no sorrow, no more tears, they have no earthly origin.

Chorus

Mark well the city, firm and strong, its gates are open all day long.
A dwelling built by God's own hand, the city of the risen Lamb.
In festal gathering there they stand, the ones he gathered with his hands.
The One who bought our liberty, the Judge who came to set us free.

Chorus

Also based on Ezekiel 37; Hebrews 11:10; 12:18–29; Revelation 21; 22.

PSALM 49: THE AIM OF MY EXISTENCE

As I sit, dear Lord, and ponder all my days and what they're worth,
Did I utilize or squander my achievements since my birth?
What's the aim of my existence and the goal for which I strive?
Am I making any difference? Do I survive or do I thrive?

Chorus
But then I look to you, my Lord, who spoke and worlds created.
At your command life took its form, began as you intended.
Yet, though you held all power and might, you chose to be a servant,
Not grasping for a crown of gold but died to buy my pardon.

There are those the world admires, they climb ladders, chase the prize,
But their dreams of wealth and stardom are not worth those sacrificed.
No ransom buys a soul its rest, nor can the grave be halted.
Both wise and foolish fade to dust, death will not be defrauded.

Chorus

Why should I fear in times of want? Why should my thoughts be anxious?
Is life not more than food and drink? To God I am not worthless.
My Father knows the things I need before I even ask him.
So, I will redirect my eyes and live to seek his kingdom.

Chorus

Lord, you're the one who saves the lost, you grant us our salvation.
The ones who trust in fleeting wealth will fall before temptation.
But treasure held in nail-scarred hands is stored for me in heaven;
The ransom paid was life for life and I am his forever.

Chorus

Also based on Matthew 6:19–34.

PSALM 50: THE LORD, THE MIGHTY ONE, HAS SPOKEN

The Lord, the Mighty One, has spoken, from dawn to dusk his voice resounds.
He shines in fire, his judgment blazing, and earth and heaven hear the sound.
He summons all before his presence, not for the gifts their hands provide.
He owns the herds on every mountain, and wants no works advanced in pride.

Chorus
So, offer now your life before him as holy and acceptable,
Be not conformed to worldly wisdom, renew your mind to do God's will.

Yet when you call, his help is near you, he rescues those who seek his name.
A heart of thanks is what he honors, a life of trust is what he claims.
But woe to those who scorn his mercy, who speak his words yet love deceit.
He sees their lies, their hollow pledges, their wicked tongues and their conceit.

Chorus

They speak of truth, yet twist its meaning, they claim his Word yet disobey.
Do they believe that God is silent? Yet he will speak to their dismay.
O searching heart, take heed and listen, whom will you seek to gratify?
The Lord desires a life surrendered, a grateful heart he'll not deny.

Chorus

Also based on Matthew 7:21–23; Romans 12:1–2.

PSALM 51: PURGE AND CLEANSE ME, O MY GOD

Have mercy on me, O my God, according to your steadfast love.
I know what my transgressions are, the sins that I am guilty of.
But you are just in all you do, your verdict stands, your word is right.
O God, have mercy, make me new. Restore my heart, redeem my life.

Chorus
Purge and cleanse me, O my God, wash me till I'm white as snow,
Fill my soul with songs of joy, let my weary bones be strong.
Hide your face from all my sin, blot out every stain I bear.
Give me a new heart, O God, do not take your life away.
Breathe in me and raise me up, guide me in your perfect way.

No wealth can buy the life I need; no sacrifice can make me clean.
No striving earns what grace has done, my hope is found in Christ alone.
His blood has paid the debt I owed; his love has broken every chain.
Now righteousness apart from law is freely given, grace remains!

Chorus

In sin I was conceived and born, to truth and wisdom I was blind.
But one has died so all may live, your love will leave no one behind.
In Jesus all has passed away, a new creation has been born.
Through Christ I have been reconciled, that which we were has been transformed.

Chorus

O God, you will not turn away from hearts that humbly seek your face.
Your mercy stands, your love remains, your power restores what sin erased.

You breathe new life where death has reigned, reviving all who trust in you. The lost are found, the broken healed, for you are faithful, good, and true!

Also based on Romans 3:21–31; 2 Corinthians 5:17–20.

PSALM 52: GOD'S OLIVE TREE

In your garden, Lord, you planted a majestic olive tree,
With its high and lofty branches bearing fruit for all to see.
But there are times when we've been battered, stormy winds have threatened life.
Deeply scarred we have been scattered, lost and weary in the night.

Chorus
O dear God, we're green and tender, prone to bend in every gale.
Ground and nurture us forever, make us stand though winds may wail.

Still your hand restores the broken, grafting in from far and near.
Called by grace we grow together, bearing fruit throughout the year.
Grow your tree, our leaves are healing for the nations tossed and twirled.
Sink our roots in your own river that our fruit may feed the world.

Chorus

Also based on Jeremiah 11:16–17; Hosea 14:6; Romans 11:17–24; Revelation 22:1–2.

PSALM 53: HELP US NOT TO BE DECEIVED

As I watch the stars I wonder: are there many, are there few?
If I cannot tell the number, do I even have a clue?
Some will claim to be decisive, saying you do not exist,
But the converse is persuasive; yet, in blindness they persist.

Chorus
What can be known of you is plain, creative power we perceive
In things we see and touch around us, help us not to be deceived.

Can one know with tight precision if there can or cannot be
One that in divine decision made the universe we see?
Can it be that their denial is logically untenable,
If their thoughts are put on trial, will they be defensible?

Chorus

So, we pray for your salvation, only you can change a heart.
Save, O Lord, from condemnation those whom you have set apart.
Open eyes that will not open; open ears that will not hear.
May they heed the words unspoken by what fills the atmosphere.

Chorus

Also based on Romans 1:19–23.

PSALM 54: YOUR FAITHFULNESS, MY CERTAINTY

O Lord, where are you when I call, for I am plagued with misery
And I am scared that I may fall; please free me from adversity.
I pray to you; are you still there? The silence lingers, dark and deep.
The night is long, my faith is weak, and all I do is wait and weep.

Chorus
But now I know that you're my helper; you uphold me through it all.
From my eyes you may seem hidden, yet you surround me like a wall
Before, behind, beside, within me. Your faithfulness, my certainty.

The fear I held was just a lie, for you, dear Lord, will never change.
Through every tear, through every trial, in you my footsteps are arranged.
No one can shake what you have built, no voice can steal what you've decreed.
So, I will trust and not be troubled, for you, my God, will never leave.

Chorus

PSALM 55: I RUN AND HIDE IN YOU

The weight is heavy, the storm won't break; my heart is trembling, my mind's awake.
The voices whisper, the night is long, I need a refuge, a place to belong.

Pre-Chorus
O the fear is loud and the pain is real, but you're the only place I can truly heal.
Chorus
If I could run, if I could hide, if I could rise above this night,
Still I'd find my heart is aching, only you can bring me light.
So, I won't run, no, I won't hide, unless I run and hide in you.

Betrayed by those I called my own, their words like daggers, I stand alone.
The city's restless, the streets are cold, but you are near, my shelter, my home.

Pre-Chorus and Chorus

Bridge
You lift me higher than fear can reach, you calm the storm inside of me.
No need to run, no need to flee, you're my escape, you set me free.

Pre-Chorus, Chorus, and Outro
So, I won't run, no, I won't hide, unless I run and hide in you.

PSALM 56: YOU HOLD MY TEARS LIKE PRECIOUS RAIN

I trusted once; I once had friends, but now I walk alone again.
Their words like daggers found their mark and left me bleeding in the dark.
They walked with me, then let me fall, I never thought they'd turn at all.
Now every step is filled with doubt, but still, my heart is crying out . . .

Pre-Chorus
O God, you see, you know my pain, you hold my tears like precious rain.
Chorus
When I'm afraid I lift my eyes, I trust in you; I won't lose sight.
Your word is sure, your love won't fail; in you my heart will rest, prevail.

The echoes of their voices ring, a shadow covers everything.
But mercy speaks with louder sound, in you my refuge now is found.

Bridge
You number all my tears, O Lord, not one is lost, not one ignored.
Through every wound, through every pain, you'll have me dancing in the rain.

Chorus and Outro
O God, you see, you know my pain, you hold my tears like precious rain . . .

PSALM 57: ABOVE THE HEAVENS

In the shadow of your wings I hide till the storms of hate subside.
Mercy flows from heaven's throne; faithful God, I'm not alone.

Pre-Chorus
I cry out loud to God Most High, he fulfills his will for me.
Chorus
Be exalted, O my God, let your glory fill the earth,
Be exalted, above the skies, let the peoples know your worth!

They try to trap me in my way, they try to make me go astray,
But you have set your love on me, so, I will sing a melody.

Pre-Chorus
Awake, my glory, harp and lyre, sing with me creation's choir.
Chorus
I will give thanks to you, O Lord, among all peoples I'll be heard.
Your love I'll praise among the nations for it is higher than the heavens.

Bridge
Your steadfast love will never fail, your faithfulness will still prevail.
My heart is steadfast, I will sing to you, my Savior, risen King.

Pre-Chorus
I cry out loud to God Most High, he fulfills his will for me.
Chorus
Be exalted, O my God, let your glory fill the earth,
Be exalted, above the skies, let the peoples know your worth!

Outro
Above the heavens, you remain, good and upright is your name.

PSALM 58: FROM EVIL, LORD, DELIVER US

Do you see their pain and sorrow? Do you hear their strangled cries?
Rulers speak, their words are hollow, agents of the lord of lies.

Pre-Chorus
Can we be silent and still claim to follow one who took our pain?
Chorus
God still reigns above the skies. His justice triumphs over lies.
Weakness stronger than the sword, truth conveyed through spoken Word.
Let your will be done on earth; from evil, Lord, deliver us.

Jesus walked the path of mercy, spoke the truth yet bore the cross.
Called us all to follow closely, deny ourselves, take up the cross.

Pre-Chorus and Chorus

Bridge
Break the chains, bring in the dawn, let the helpless know they're not alone.
Lift the lowly, shake the proud, let your justice thunder loud!

Chorus and Outro
Let your will be done on earth; from evil, Lord, deliver us.

PSALM 59: YOU ARE KING DESPITE IT ALL

I lie awake at dead of night, my swirling thoughts I cannot fight.
The world is shattered, nations groan, I strain to see you on your throne.
Depression lurks behind the door, and sneers that hope is mine no more.
The weight of sorrow drags me down, and I'm afraid that I might drown.

Pre-Chorus
I am confused, my Lord, and dazed; my doubts and fears still gnaw and rage,
They prowl, they snarl, they fill the air with echoes of my own despair.
How long, O Lord, till morning breaks? For answered prayer I wail and wait.
Chorus
But I will sing once I regain my faith amid this doubt and pain.
I lift my eyes to you, my strength, I know that evil will be quenched.
At present, I don't see it all, but I see him who bore it all.

The cities burn, the children weep, the hungry die, the helpless plead.
Where is the promise of your reign? Why do I feel so lost and drained?
Confusion numbs, my heartache bleeds, my prayers fall like the autumn leaves.
I long to see your kingdom come, the rule of Christ the risen Son.

Pre-Chorus and Chorus

Bridge
You sat down at your Father's hand till all submit to your command.
Till nothing evil still remains, then peace and love will finally reign.

Chorus
So, I will sing once I regain my faith amid this doubt and pain.
I lift my eyes to you, my strength, I know that evil will be quenched.
At present, I don't see it all, but I see him who bore it all.

Outro
So, in the dark I will recall that you are King despite it all . . .

Also based on 1 Corinthians 15:24–25; Hebrews 2:8–9.

PSALM 60: I KNOW THAT THE BATTLE'S WON

O God, have you rejected me? I'm broken and in misery.
My life once shone with golden blaze, but now it's turned to ashen haze.
The earth beneath me shakes and starts, the sky above seems torn apart.
I stumble and don't understand. Am I abandoned in the dark?

Pre-Chorus
The shadows whisper, "Hope is gone," but I know that the battle's won.
Chorus
I lift my eyes to see the cross, and I take courage, all's not lost.
Just like a banner plain to see, your death ensures my victory.

For now, my life's like bitter wine as circumstances weigh me down.
I'm vulnerable and breakable, it won't take much for me to drown.
O help me Lord, and turn to me, for none on earth can set me free.
With God I shall do valiantly, he will tread down my enemy.

Pre-Chorus and Chorus

Bridge
You have not left, you have not failed, your covenant of love prevails.
The risen Christ, the empty grave, my mighty Savior strong to save.

Chorus and Outro
The shadows whisper, "Hope is gone," but I know that the battle's won.

PSALM 61: HIGHER THAN I

When institutions crash and fail, when every plan falls through,
When wealth and power fade away and debts are overdue,
When wars erupt, dictators rule, when angry words are hurled,
Where can I turn, where can I find assurance in this world?

My life keeps shifting under me, like waves upon the sand.
The things I trusted let me down, I cannot understand.
No structure or arrangement on earth can satisfy,
So, lead me to the rock, dear Lord, the rock higher than I.

Chorus
You are my shelter, you're my strength, you're my security and peace,
You are the home where I belong, you are my heritage increased.

Your mercy's never limited, your truth will never fade,
Throughout the ages and beyond your promises remain.
Though nations rise and fall apart, their glory fades and dies,
So, keep me on the rock, dear Lord, the rock higher than I.

Bridge
The wealth we chase will vanish, investments stop and start,
But Christ, the firm foundation, preserves my restless heart.
No fear can shake this refuge, no storm can tear it down,
For on a higher rock I stand, stable, safe, and sound.

Chorus and Outro
So, keep me on the rock, dear Lord, the rock higher than I.

PSALM 62: O GOD, MY REFUGE, STRONG AND SURE

Chorus
O God, my refuge, strong and sure, in you my hope remains secure.
You are my fortress, firm and great, my soul shall rest; I'll trust and wait.

In peace I wait on God alone, my rock, my strong foundation stone.
When troubles rise, I shall not fear, for he is close, his help is near.
Though enemies may press me down, my God upholds my victor's crown.
Their strength is fleeting, weak as dust, but God remains my hope and trust.

Chorus

Bridge
Wait in silence, O my soul, all remains in his control.
Wait, hope, rest; wait, hope, rest.

Pour out your hearts, O people near, to him who knows your every fear.
His steadfast love shall never fail, a refuge strong through every gale.
Not wealth nor power can make us whole, for God alone redeems our soul.
In him is power, love, and peace, from age to age, his care won't cease.

Chorus

PSALM 62: FOR GOD ALONE MY SOUL IS WAITING

Chorus
For God alone my soul is waiting, from him comes my deliverance.
He is my fortress and my stronghold, my solid rock, my sure defence.

How long will you attack the weary; like crumbling walls, they barely stand.
The helpless drown in waves of fury. Do none extend a saving hand?
Our leaders speak with words deceiving, uttering lies they claim to bless.
Yet in their hearts they plot in secret, their treachery they'll not confess.

Chorus

On God alone my soul is waiting, my refuge strong, my mighty shield.
I lift my cries, my sad lamenting. When, dear Lord, will all be healed?
The lowly rise, the mighty stumble, both fleeting flashes in the air.
Their lives are short before they crumble to rise as vapor in despair.

Chorus

Bridge
Once you have spoken, twice I've heard: All power, Lord, belongs to you.
Yet greater still your steadfast love, your justice pure, your judgment true.

Don't chase success or trust in stealing, ill-gotten wealth or stashed reserves.
If riches grow, don't let them capture the place that only God deserves.

Chorus and Outro
For God alone my soul is waiting, from him comes my deliverance

PSALM 63: YOUR LOVE IS MORE THAN LIFE

Lord, I'm thirsty, dehydrated; I'm in need of sustenance
For my soul is dry and empty, I have lost all confidence.
As I wait I look to Jesus, there I know that I will find
Trust becomes pure adoration, leaving doubt and fear behind.

Chorus
Because your love is more than life, more than the sweetness of the light,
I lift my hands, and with my mouth I'll sing your praises through the night.

You satisfy my thirsting soul, with richest feast you feed me,
And in the shadow of your wings I cling to you completely.
I think on you while on my bed, through nights, I will remember,
I meditate upon your Word, my refuge and defender.

Chorus

Bridge
I will not fear, I will not fall, you are my shelter, you're my all.
And in the deserts you are near, Lord Jesus, you are always here.

Chorus and Outro
My lips will praise, my soul will sing, you are my God, my everything.

PSALM 64: RISING, YOU DESTROYED DESPAIR

Hear my voice, O Lord, in mercy; the world is veiled in dark disguise
Where whispers wound and gossips lie, where fabrication blurs the lines.
The proud conspire, they plot and plan, they weave their snares in secret ways.
And truth is trampled in the cause, and righteousness and justice fade.

Chorus
But you, O Lord, have borne the pain, the sin we shaped you chose to bear.
Destructive powers you disarmed and rising, you destroyed despair.

No sudden fury rights the wrong, no blast of justice clears the dross.
As mercy moves your loving heart, your power perfected at the cross.

Bridge
The empty tomb, the risen King, the hope that will not fade away.
Your justice dawns, your kingdom comes, a light no dark can disregard.

Chorus

Also based on 1 Corinthians 1:25; 2 Corinthians 12:9–10; Colossians 2:13–15.

PSALM 65: YOUR RIVER RUNS WITH MERCY

O Lord, to you my songs arise, in silence and in vows,
For every heart that turns to you forgiveness shall be found.
Though heavy weighs the debt I owe, you lift my sins away,
You call me near, you hold me fast, and bless me day by day.

Chorus
Your river runs with mercy, the hills break forth in song,
The valleys laugh with golden grain as showers roll along.
O God, you crown the seasons with love so full and free,
The earth and sky together sing in wondrous ecstasy.

You calm the roaring of the seas, the waves that rise and crash,
The nations hear your thunderous voice and see the lightening flash.
From dawn to dusk, from dusk to dawn, you set the sky ablaze,
And in the hush of evening's glow the earth presents its praise.

Chorus

You bless the fields with gentle rain, the pastures rich and deep,
The rivers run, the harvest sings, and joy stirs in our sleep.
The meadows bloom in flowers white, the hills with gladness ring,
And every breath of life proclaims the goodness of our King.

Chorus

PSALM 66: FROM DEATH TO LIFE

Shout for joy to God Most High! Sing the glory of his name!
Give to him all wondrous praise, awesome deeds we must proclaim!
All the earth come and witness, see him split the sea in two
And the river like dry land, passing through them both on foot.

Chorus
Come and see, join us in worship, all the earth come sing for joy;
From death to life the Lord has brought us, through his death, death is destroyed.

Once he led them in their flight, a fire by day, a cloud by night.
But now our Lord has split the grave, names upon his palms engraved.
I will tell of what he's done through his mercy, through his Son.
By his sacrifice for all, he undid the cursed Fall.

Chorus

Bridge
He has tested, he has tried, silver purified in fire.
He has brought us to this place, the abundance of his grace.
Truly God has heard my prayers, he has not removed from me
Steadfast loving kindnesses: come all peoples, come and see.

Chorus

PSALM 67: LET THE PEOPLES PRAISE YOUR NAME

May God be gracious, bless us all, and make his face shine through the storms.
Reveal his ways in every sphere, his saving power from year to year.

Pre-Chorus
Let all the hungry find their bread and all the weary raise their heads.
Chorus
Let the peoples praise you, Lord, let all the peoples praise you.
From the mountains to the seas let there be peace and harmony.

The gulf between the rich and poor, injustice and indifference,
Their cries are heard from shore to shore, please judge the world in righteousness.

Pre-Chorus and Chorus

For then the earth will yield its grain and deserts drink the summer rain,
Then every soul will find its home and call our Shepherd theirs alone.

Pre-Chorus, Chorus, and Outro
Let your blessings make us whole that the world may see and know
You, dear Lord, are on your throne, no one needs to be alone.

Also based on Genesis 12:1–3; Numbers 6:22–27.

PSALM 68: SUMMON YOUR POWER, O KING OF THE SKIES

Intro
God shall arise, all evil be scattered as smoke on the breeze, as wax by the flames,
Like rocks by the waves are battered and bashed; his march will continue till all know his name.

Let the clouds break, let the winds rise, let the storms rage through thunderous skies.
He sweeps through the deserts like eagles on high, he sees every tear and hears every cry.
The righteous shall stand and they shall rejoice, firmly established they'll lift up their voice,
Look to the heavens, sing praise to his name. They'll dance in the sunlight, and laugh in the rain.

Chorus
Summon your power, O King of the skies, thunder your justice and fire in your eyes.
Father to orphans and home to the lost, for every mortal you've carried the cross.

The prisoners walk, their chains left behind, the song of the free now the song of mankind.
You shake every mountain, you water the land, your blessings advance as your kingdom expands.

Chorus

Bridge
Who is like you, O God, wrapped in the storm?
Who speaks and the deserts are clothed in the dawn?
Who rides on the clouds, who calls us his own?
Who smashes the strongholds, who leads us all home?

The planet is trembling, the rivers run wide, the mighty are falling, the meek you will guide.
Your voice is a whisper, a flame in the night, a promise unbroken, a pillar of light.
A message is heard from the mountain of God, the captives are freed by the hands scarred with love.
Strengthen your people, your goodness restore, scatter the peoples that delight in war.

Chorus and Outro
God shall arise, all evil be scattered as smoke on the breeze, as wax by the flames,
Like rocks by the waves are battered and bashed; his march will continue till all know his name.

PSALM 69: THE FLOOD IS RISING

Alone beneath the olive branches, he fell in silence to the ground,
His hands were trembling, he sweat in fear, the weight of sorrow dragged him down.
The flood was rising, pulling him under, he sank where solid ground gave way.
He prayed for mercy, but all were sleeping, his throat was raw, his strength like sand.
The hate was heavy, the plots were violent, they sought his life without a cause.
He bore the debt he never borrowed, he drank the cup and fulfilled the law.

Chorus
But the Father heard his crying, saw the darkness closing in.
He had loved him but decided that his blood must cleanse my sin.

He'd been a stranger to his brothers, a foreign voice in his own home.
He burned with zeal to cleanse the temple, now he was left to bleed alone.
They laughed and mocked, they gave him gall and turned his thirst to bitter wine.
They cursed the wounds he took upon him, they shook their heads and closed their eyes.

Chorus

Bridge
So, I will trust you in my breaking, the grave will not hold back the dawn.
The ones who seek you do not falter; they will be saved; they will live on.
Let the poor find hope before you, let the captives rise and sing.
For, though I fall, you will not leave me, you are my God, my everything.

Chorus and Outro
The flood is rising, pulling me under, but you will lift me up again.

PSALM 70: DO NOT DELAY, DO NOT FORSAKE

The weight is pressing heavy now, my mind is plagued with doubt,
I whisper prayers into the dark, my soul is crying out.
My voice is lost in empty air, my hands reach up in vain;
O God who hears the weary soul, reach down and ease my pain.

Chorus
Please, come in time, come in power, turn the tide, redeem the hour.
Do not delay, do not forsake, O Lord, I am about to break.

Uncertainty erodes my hope, perhaps you've closed a door,
Perhaps the ones who cry too long aren't welcome anymore.
But justice shines beyond distress, like dawn behind a hill,
And though the waiting burns like fire, I trust you hear me still.

Chorus

Bridge
Like the widows and the orphans, like the helpless in their chains,
Like the child, lost and wandering, calling out their parents' names
I am pleading, I am waiting, though the night is deep and wide,
I believe that you are faithful, you are always by my side.

Chorus and Outro
The weight is pressing heavy now, the night is thick with doubt,
But I will sing into the dark; my soul keeps crying out.
Do not delay, do not forsake . . .

PSALM 71: CONCEPTION THROUGH TO RESURRECTION

You took me from my mother's womb, before my birth you knew my name.
But now before me looms the tomb, don't cast me off in my old age.
From infancy you've taught me grace, I still proclaim your wondrous deeds.
Through every trial that I have faced you have supplied my every need.

Pre-Chorus
From day to day, throughout the years, my heart will trust as you are near.
Chorus
I won't be anxious for my life; you have carried me this far.
All my days are in your keeping, every wound and every scar.
So, I'll praise you in the morning and when twilight fades to dusk.
Conception through to resurrection, I remain unshaken in my trust.

Bridge
Look at the lilies, how they grow, dressed in a beauty not their own.
Look at the sparrow, unafraid, trusting in provision made.
Why should I doubt? Why should I fear? Your hand has led me all these years.

And now my hair is turning gray, O God, do not forsake me
Until your power I've proclaimed to another generation.
You've made me face calamities yet revived me every time.
O my God, none stands beside you, in your greatness you're sublime.

Pre-Chorus, Chorus, and Outro
Conception through to resurrection, I remain unshaken in my trust.

PSALM 72: HE SHALL ENDURE

O may our King in justice rule, in righteousness judge all the land.
May all do well under his hand and all thrive under his command.
May he defend the poor and weak, deliver those who have been wronged.
Like rain upon the thirsty fields, may peace abound and be prolonged.

Pre-Chorus
Through endless days and years unknown he shall endure upon his throne.
Chorus
Blessed be the Lord, the God of grace, who can alone do wondrous things.
Blessed be his glorious name always; may all on earth his praises sing!

From sea to sea his reign shall spread, his kingdom through the universe.
All mortal leaders bring their gifts as blessings cleanse and purge the curse.
He saves the needy when they call, he helps the hopeless in their plight.
The blood of those oppressed and weak is counted precious in his sight.

Pre-Chorus and Chorus

Bridge
The wolf and lamb shall live in peace, the leopard lie beside the goat.
The lion and the calf composed, and a little child shall lead them.
May his name shine like the sun, a blessing to all clans and tongues.
And may the nations lift their voices to praise the name of Christ the Son.

Pre-Chorus, Chorus, and Outro
Forever shall his name endure, through every age, his reign secure.

Also based on Isaiah 11:6.

BOOK THREE

Psalms 73–89

PSALM 73: WHOM HAVE I IN HEAVEN BUT YOU?

Intro
O Lord, will you direct my eyes, not on the evil that abounds,
But let me see you on your throne and let me know I'm not alone.

I looked around, what did I see? The wicked rise, the weary weep.
I let their treasures cloud my sight, I almost stumbled in my plight.

Pre-Chorus
But then I turned to you and saw and, in your presence, I was awed.
For now, I see the end they'll face as we all stand secure in grace.

Chorus
Whom have I in heaven but you? Nothing else on earth will do.
My heart may fail, my flesh grow weak, but you, my God, are all I seek.

I let my soul be filled with doubt, I thought that you had cast me out.
But like the shadows flee at dawn, my anxious fears are now all gone.

Bridge
You are my portion, you're my prize, forever near, forever wise.
I once was blind but now I see, you are my strength and destiny.

Chorus and Outro
Though the cruel may rise and fall, still, my God, you're Lord of all.
Ever faithful, ever true, all I need is found in you.

PSALM 74: ARISE, O GOD!

O God, where are you in my need? Why does the darkness close me in?
My burdens rise like fire and ash, tearing down the walls within.
Fears roar within my quiet space, mad woodsmen in my peaceful grove.
They break the altars of my faith, scattering embers, crushing hope.

Pre-Chorus
Yet you have called me as your own, your hands have never let me go.
Chorus
Arise, O God, defend your cause! Do not forget and do not pause.
My faith in you I do proclaim, do not let me be put to shame.

You calmed the sea, you stilled the waves, yours is the day, yours is the night.
You fixed the boundaries of the earth; you made the spheres that give us light.

Pre-Chorus and Chorus

Bridge
Direct your steps to see my ruin, see what the enemy's destroyed.
And yet my God is Lord of all, he will not let his children fall.

Pre-Chorus and Outro
Arise, O God, I trust your ways, your light will drive my night away.
I know your mercy will not fade, forever you remain the same.
Because you have called me as your own, your hands will never let me go.

PSALM 74: YOU KNOW THE TRUTH, LORD, AND JUSTICE IS DUE

They came in the night like a thief in the dark, tanks rolling like thunder, ashen and stark.
Our houses are burning, our children have fled, the streets we once danced in are shattered and shred.
They marched like a flood through the fields and the plains, tearing up lives like immense hurricanes.
They carved up the land like a butcher at trade while the world stood indifferent, our allies afraid.

Chorus
O Lord, do you see? O Lord, do you hear? *The cries of the broken still ring in the air.*
They say we are nothing, they say we are through, but you know the truth, Lord, and justice is due.

They speak in assemblies with lies on their breath, blaming the battered for fighting till death.
They broker for peace and shake empty hands while selling our sorrow for minerals and land.
The friends we once trusted now turn from our door, they balance their ledgers; they're counting the score.
They say we're not grateful and ask for too much, but they will increase while we live in the dust.

Chorus

Bridge
Bombs are exploding and missiles are flying; our sons and our daughters are bleeding and dying.

We beg and we plead, we grovel and bow, but those we once trusted have broken their vows.

The ashes still fall as the rain turns to black, the dead and the stolen will never come back.
But the night isn't endless, the dawn will soon come, the battle's not over till victory's won.

Chorus

Dedicated to the brave people of Ukraine.
Also based on 2 Kings 24–25; 2 Chronicles 36; Psalm 137:7; Lamentations 2:15–16; Ezekiel 25:3–14; 26:2; Obadiah 1:10–14.

PSALM 75: THE CUP OF THE ALMIGHTY

O the halls of the high and their mansions of gold, they glitter and shine, but their hearts have been sold.
They laugh in their chambers, they toast to their schemes, but the Judge of the earth isn't blind to their dreams.

Chorus
The earth and the heavens are firm in his hand, he executes judgment, obedience demands;
He holds up the cup and he pours out the wine, the wicked will drink down his fury in time.

They speak of their power, they boast in their pride, they trample the weary, they cast truth aside.
But when the earth totters, the mighty fall down, and the Lord of all justice will shatter their crowns.

Chorus

Bridge
O the strength of the wicked will snap like dry reeds, but the lowly will rise like the tall cedar trees.
For the promise of God isn't slow, isn't weak, in mercy he's patient, but soon he will speak.

Give thanks to your Maker, recount all his deeds, for he is well able your prayers to exceed.
The proud and the haughty are pawns in his hands, unwitting, their evil fulfils his commands.

Chorus and Outro
O the halls of the high and their mansions of gold, they glitter and shine, but their hearts have been sold.
For the Judge of all nations sees through all their lies, the conceited will fall, but the righteous shall rise.

Also based on Ephesians 3:20–21; 2 Peter 3:9.

PSALM 76: YOUR NAME IS GREAT AND WONDROUS

You're more glorious than the sunlight, than majestic mountain peaks.
You remain beyond description, in your beauty you're complete.

Pre-Chorus
Who can stand against your anger? Who can rise against your hand?
You have shattered bows and armies, saved the humble of the land.
Chorus
For your name is great and wondrous, your magnificence sublime.
You are holy in your justice and in mercy you're divine.

You're the firstborn of creation for by you all things exist.
You're the author of salvation and in you my life persists.

Pre-Chorus
Who could fathom such a wonder? The Almighty bends so low!
For he laid my sins upon you that the guilty one might go.
Chorus

For in you I am forgiven, you have cancelled all my debt.
You disarmed satanic forces, triumphed over all their threats.

Bridge
You were pierced and crushed in anguish as the curse fell on your frame.
In the place where I lay broken you have borne my grief and shame.

Chorus

Also based on Galatians 3:13–14; Colossians 1:15–20; 2:14–15.

PSALM 77: YOU ARE HERE AS YOU WERE THERE

I cry out in silence, but no answer comes, nights stretch on forever, and my soul feels numb.
I reach for the heavens, and wait for the day, my God, do you hear me? How long must I wait?
I consider the stories, the wonders you've done, how you intervened, and how victories were won.
But now in my troubles I'm lost in my fear, I can't help but wonder, will you still appear?

Pre-Chorus
Have you turned away? Have you closed your hand? Where are you, O Lord, I can't understand.
Chorus
But Lord, you were there when creation began, you gathered the waters and made the dry land.
With fire and thunder, with mercy and might, you led and you guided through every night.
And if you were there, then you're still here with me, and so, you'll be with me for eternity.

I walk through the echoes of battles long past, your presence was with them, your hands held them fast.
I look to the cross and consider your joy, erasure of debt as the curse was destroyed.

Pre-Chorus
No, you haven't changed, and you never will, your love is a river that keeps flowing still.
Chorus

Yes Lord, you were there when creation began, you gathered the waters and made the dry land.
With fire and thunder, with mercy and might, you led and you guided through every night.
And if you were there, then you're still here with me, and so, you'll be with me for eternity.

I think and I ponder on him who endured such hated aggression that I'd be secure.
Then how can I waver and weaken in faith? No, I will press on and I'll finish my race.

Bridge
So, I will remember, I'll hold to your name, through storm and through silence, you still are the same.
You still walk before me, you still part the sea, the God of the ages is walking with me.

Chorus
Yes, Lord, you were there when creation began, you gathered the waters and made the dry land.
With fire and thunder, with mercy and might, you led and you guided through every night.
And if you were there, then you're still here with me, and so, you'll be with me for eternity.

Outro
So, now in the silence I ponder and know that, even in darkness, I'm never alone.

Also based on Hebrews 12:2–3.

PSALM 78: WE WILL TELL THE STORY

This is a story of our Lord's great might and how he worked to put the world to rights,
One that will echo through all time, give us a different paradigm
Through which to study history and that enables us to see
The saving of the world.

Chorus
We will tell the story of what God has done that all generations that are yet to come
Will know how he took us from darkness to light, released us from bondage and set us upright,
Guided and made us all sheep of his flock, established us firmly upon the rock.

Taken from Egypt by his mighty hand, opened the sea and caused the waves to stand.
He gave them water and their bread; however, when they all were fed
They built an idol, worshipped stars; and, even though it seems bizarre,
He loved and still forgave.

Chorus

But then a greater and a deeper night, our Lord and Savior won for us the fight
Against the curse that held us all, in detention since the Fall.
His blood has torn the veil away and has opened up the way
For us to live with him.

Chorus

And now the call booms like a trumpet blast, the cursed serpent's head is crushed at last.
He broke the chains of sin and death so that we may be given rest
And share his own life-giving breath with every soul from east to west
And witness to his love.

Chorus and Outro
This was the story of our Lord's great might and how he worked to put the world to rights,
But it's not over till he comes again, and so, he guides us with his skilful hand
To tell his story to the world.

Also based on Matthew 28:18–20.

PSALM 79: FORGIVE AND CLEANSE AND MAKE ME NEW

Dear Father, would you shine your light into this crazy life of mine?
There are some things that aren't quite right, please would you pull me back in line?
Neglect and my indifference and my offenses said and done,
Wrongdoing and forgetfulness, the good things I have left undone.

Chorus
These sins and sins I have forgot, Almighty God, I bring to you,
I confess and seek your pardon, forgive and cleanse and make me new.

And so, we come, your sheep, O Lord, to you, our Shepherd; we implore
Forgive and free us from our sin, and through your Spirit, heal within.

For now our battle's fought and won through Jesus your beloved Son.
By grace and mercy, set us free, absolve and heal us, Lord, we plead.

Chorus and Outro
We humbly bow as we receive the cleansing only you can give.
So, thank you Jesus, risen Son; I rise, refreshed, my guilt is gone.
Amen.

PSALM 80: THE PRAYER OF THE PERSECUTED CHURCH

Give ear, O my Shepherd, hear the cries of your flock.
Enthroned above angels, seated firm like a rock,
Shine forth in your glory, and summon your strength,
How long till you answer? Come save us again.

You fed us with bread that was made from our tears,
Your silence continues despite all our prayers.
You've made us an object of laughter and scorn.
Our enemies mock us as we weep and mourn.

Chorus
O Lord, will you bless? O Lord, will you keep?
The enemy murders and slaughters your sheep.
O Lord, make your face to shine and transcend,
Be gracious and grant us your peace once again.

They came with their torches, their axes were sharp,
They burned all our churches and left in the dark.
This vine that you planted, which grew big and strong,
They ravaged and pillaged and dragged it along.

O Lord, though we walk through deep valleys of pain,
In smouldering ashes, we cry out your name.
O Lord God of hosts, please look down from your throne,
Observe all your children, don't leave us alone!

Chorus

Bridge
But you, Lord, are ruling, your enemies scatter,
Your children are dying and they are what matter

Rebuke them and save us, O Lord, make us stand
Revive us and lift us once more by your hand.

Chorus and Outro
Our Savior and Shepherd do not pass us by.
Restore us and lift us, O Lord, hear our cries.

Also based on Numbers 6:24–26.

PSALM 81: IF ONLY WE'D LISTEN

They sang in the glow of the full harvest moon, they told all their stories, an old, borrowed tune.
Of how they were rescued, when God split the sea, and how they were cared for once they all were free.
God gave them commandments, out of thunder he spoke in flashes of fire, the mountain of smoke.
He fed them from heaven, gave water from stone, but they turned away, followed rules of their own.

Pre-Chorus
Still, voices entice us to lead us astray, and yet God is calling, submit and obey.
Chorus
If only we'd listen, if only we'd hear, the Lord God would bless us and keep us all near
So that we'd be safer and no longer fear. Our foes he would vanquish, supply all our needs,
The very best honey, the finest of wheat, his table of plenty, his words and decrees.

Still, we are distracted by gods of this age, our phones and our tablets, whatever's the rage.
The voices of media demand we comply; we fill all our hours; our spirits run dry.
We wanted it easy, so we forged our chains, we wanted our freedom, to loosen restraints.
And we called it progress; we said we were free; but we must examine, ask what we believe.

Pre-Chorus and Chorus

Bridge
Not in the storm, not in the fire, not in the rush of the world's desire.
But in the whisper that comes on a breeze, the one who still loves you beckons and pleads.

Chorus

PSALM 82: THE JUDGE AT THE TABLE

The hall was lit by chandeliers, the table decked with gold,
The leaders spoke with lying tongues, their faces hard and cold.
Then came a voice like rolling thunder, shaking every seat,
And every head was turned to see who dared disrupt their feast.

"I see unequal weights on scales, dishonesty, and more.
But tell me now, you men of law, who speaks up for the poor?
How long will you defend the thieves, let murderers go free,
Embolden more ungodly men to keep all on their knees?"

Chorus
Arise, O Lord, and take the throne, the earth is yours to reign,
No tyrant's law, no liar's tongue, should mock your name again.
The nations groan beneath the weight of men who cheat and steal;
Arise, O Lord, and break the chains, let truth and mercy heal.

They sipped their wine and gave a grin, said, "God, who gave you leave?
We deal in laws and governance; your words we don't believe."
God struck the table with his hand and every lamp grew dim.
"The widow weeps, the orphan starves: their lives are short and grim.

"Protect the low, defend the weak, let no more blood be shed,
For justice is not bought with bribes, nor righteousness with dread.
Your words are wind, your wisdom blind, you walk a darkened path,
You build on sand and think it stone, but soon you'll know my wrath."

Chorus

The ceiling groaned, the floorboards creaked, the table cracked in two,
The leaders clutched their reeling seats, unsure of what to do.

"You think yourselves as mighty gods, but gods you'll never be,
For like the poor you trample down, you too will finally grieve."

Chorus

PSALM 83: DO NOT BE SILENT

The winds of war rattle my shutters and clouds gather under red skies.
The wicked advance by their legions with genocide firm in their minds.
They whisper their plans in the darkness, to tear us apart and destroy,
Their aim is to leave no survivors, to rape and to plunder and spoil.

Chorus
O God, don't be silent, please, don't turn away. Arise like a fire and surge like a storm,
Prevent them and stop them and make them obey. Please scatter the wicked that they may conform.

As tumbleweed blown in the desert, like chaff blown away in the wind,
O drive them away as defeated and censured by your discipline.
I've read all the stories of triumph, the proud you brought down to the ground.
You fought for those you called your children, restoring a peace that abounds.

Chorus

But Father, in your tender mercy, convict them of sin and offense
And cause them to ask for your pardon and experience your magnificence.
May every tribe, tongue, and nation be bonded together in love
That arrogance, war, and destruction be ended and all be resolved.

Chorus

PSALM 84: WE MEET YOU IN YOUR GRANDEUR

O my Father, how I hunger for that great and glorious space
Where the faithful and the humble come to meet you face-to-face.
You're my source of joy and worship, you're my radiant burning light,
How I long to stand before you, for your splendor's my delight.

How the sages through the ages tried to tell of what they saw
In their moments of disclosure of the visions they foresaw;
Gates of pearl and streets all golden, pure, refined as clear as glass,
And the glory of your presence and your river flowing past.

Chorus
Who is like you, O my Father? Who is like you, blessed Son?
Who is like you Holy Spirit? Who is like the Three-in-One?
For the space in which we worship is designed for but one thing,
That we meet you in your grandeur, O our great and wondrous King!

So, in boldness we approach you, as we have a great High Priest
Who has risen and ascended and is seated on the throne.
In his grace he has invited all the humble to his feast
And has seated at his table all the sheep within his fold.

For we do not come in darkness, nor approach in gloom or storm,
But to heaven's vibrant city where the firstborn are enrolled,
And to Jesus our Redeemer, Mediator, Savior, Friend.
Joining angels and archangels, in your presence we ascend.

Chorus

For one day spent in your presence is far better than elsewhere.
Let me serve you as your servant in your kingdom anywhere.
For Lord, you are my sunlight, you're my great protective shield,
You confer upon the righteous all that wholesomeness can yield.

Chorus

Also based on Hebrews 4:14–16; 12:18–24; Revelation 21; 22.

PSALM 85: REVIVE US, RESTORE US

Intro
Revive us, restore us, so we might rejoice and praise you and bless you with music and voice.

By the tree in the garden the whisperer came, and into her ear he mentioned your name.
"Did God really say that you'll surely die?" And so he continued to fabricate lies.
Discarding the truth, they did what was wrong and banished themselves from the presence of God.
But even in judgment, of mercy you spoke, the Son of the Virgin would fix what they broke.

Chorus
By the tree in the garden the Lamb of God sealed our freedom from sin and the sentence repealed.
And there in his mercy, the judgment consigned, he cancelled as rightness and truth intertwined.

And so, you forgave us and covered our sin, withdrew from your anger, restored us again.
But Lord we have wandered, again gone astray, and need you to lead us all back to your way.
Revive us, restore us, so we might rejoice and praise you and bless you with music and voice.
Let love and salvation, your mercy and peace, flow down from your throne so that sin might decrease.

Chorus and Outro
Revive us, restore us, so we might rejoice and praise you and bless you with music and voice.

Also based on Genesis 3; Colossians 2:13–14.

PSALM 86: YOU ALONE ARE MY GOD

I come before you empty handed, in poorness of spirit and lost.
I've lived to do all you commanded; I've trusted and counted the cost.
Be gracious to me, O my Father, to you all my prayers will ascend.
Preserve me and gladden my spirit and come to my side to defend.

Chorus
Who is like you? Who can compare? There is no one I could find anywhere.
No one is greater; no one more wondrous. So, teach me O Lord, you are my compass,
You alone are my God.

For you, Lord, are good and forgiving, abounding in love and in grace.
Please hear me as one of your children, enfold me in tender embrace.
So, turn and give strength to your servant, for only you can make me whole.
You're merciful, steadfast, and glorious, the one who delivered my soul.

Chorus

Please show me a sign of your favor, let enemies all be ashamed.
May nations bow down and acclaim you and glorify your precious name.

Chorus

PSALM 87: GOD'S CITY OF LIGHT

Above the heavens God has founded this holy city for his own,
Where Jesus is our Mediator through whom we have our timeless home.
I hear the sound of rushing waters; I see the walls of jewels shine.
The gates stand open for the nations, this holy ground where love is life.

Pre-Chorus
All our names are written here, born again in love and grace.
Dwelling place of God with us, we behold him face-to-face.
Chorus
Heavenly City, God's City of Light, the River of Life flows along deep and bright,
And on its embankment the Tree of Life stands, its leaves are for healing, with life from his hands.
All tears have been banished, all darkness is past, the one who has conquered is seated at last.

No need for sun, no need for temple, the Lamb is shining from his throne.
Our heritage cannot be shaken, here all the faithful find their home.

Pre-Chorus and Chorus

Bridge
Like a bride adorned and ready, we reveal the grace of God,
Radiating all the glory, shining from our risen Lord.

Chorus

Also based on Hebrews 12:18–24; Revelation 21:1—22:5.

PSALM 88: THE PRICE HAS BEEN PAID

Well, I'm not surprised to find myself here again,
Seems like a long-lost friend's here to meet me, but then
I've cried out to you more than I care to admit, but here I am back in the pit,
I'm not sure what to do.

I feel so shut in and it seems that there is no escape,
Eyes swollen shut from the tears I have copiously shed.
You seem to be angry with me and I feel so alone, have you just cast me aside?
Or am I blind to your light?

Chorus
My fears rise and fall, and they engulf me each day.
The waves and the currents are strong, and I can't find the shore.
O God, are you hiding? O please tell me, are you still there?
If yes, well then don't pass me by. Do you still hear my cries?

My soul's full of troubles, and I have no more strength to defend.
So, where is that steadfast love that I've known in the past?
You're my salvation, O Lord, and I know you're my God, so, I will wait for you,
For whom else can I trust?

My closest companions appear to me to be darkness and night,
But I can't even put up a fight, they just wash over me.
Yet mercy still lingers, so please, will you come to my aid? I know there's a price to be paid
But that was paid at the cross.

PSALM 89: THE KING WHO REIGNS

Our walls are smashed, our gates are burned, the throne of David overturned.
Our leaders are all bound in chains, are dragged through foreign streets in shame.
We sang of love that never fails, of promises that must prevail.
But now invasion drowns our song, how could our God have got it wrong?

Did not his voice divide the sea?
Did not his hand set captives free?
Yet now his chosen ones seem lost,
A kingdom crushed at such a cost.

Chorus
How long, O sovereign God and Lord, will evil triumph with the sword?
And yet by faith we see your throne, our glorious King and Cornerstone.

We stood beneath that brutal tree, and as we watched, all we could see
Was our Messiah and our Friend come to a grim and bitter end.
This man who once had fed the poor, who claimed to be our open door,
Who said the kingdom was at hand . . . we simply couldn't understand.

We thought he'd reign with iron might, we thought he'd set the world to rights.
Now silence fills the empty air, and God himself seems unaware.

Chorus

You claimed that all authority was given to our risen Lord,
And that he reigns in sovereignty, to bring all evil to the floor.
But powers rage and nations scheme, they sell us lies and kill our dreams.
The halls of justice rot within, while all that's good remains hidden.

And yet in opposition you are seen to reign and to renew.
For in our weakness, we believe God's promises will be achieved.

Bridge
The throne of David still will stand, though everything seems out of hand.
The King ascended wears the crown, all enemies will be cast down.

Chorus

Also based on Hebrews 2:8–9.

BOOK FOUR

Psalms 90–106

PSALM 90: TEACH US TO NUMBER OUR DAYS

I stood at the graveside and watched as the pallbearers shovelled in dirt;
And as I was standing and watching, I wondered, Why does it still hurt?
The mourners soon huddled and gathered together to pay their respects.
From ashes to ashes, and all were reminded that life ends in death.

Chorus
For every stage of our lives, Lord, your grace and your presence's been there.
From time immemorial your love and your kindness have been everywhere.
For even before you created the mountains and seas had been made,
To each generation your dwelling place with us had been prearranged.

The years of our life will soon vanish, as now and then we pass along.
So, teach us to number our days as you give us a heart of wisdom.
And satisfy us every morning with whispers of loving embrace.
Please make us all glad for as many days as you've already erased.

Chorus

So, show to your children the wonderful, marvellous works of your hands,
Your glorious power to each generation so they'll understand
That favour and blessing should never be taken for granted at all,
That you alone prosper the given vocations to which we've been called.

Chorus

PSALM 91: SHELTERED IN HIS SHADOW

The night falls hard, and silence burns where voices used to be,
A hollow space where laughter stood now echoes back at me.
The weight of sorrow wraps around, a heavy, unseen chain,
I close my eyes, but even dreams can't wash away the pain.

I hear the whispers in the dark, the fears I dare not name,
They speak of all that's lost to dust, of ruin, guilt, and shame.
Yet somewhere deep within my chest, I hear another voice:
A voice that says all is not lost, that I may yet rejoice.

Pre-Chorus
Beneath the grief, beneath the ache, a quiet truth remains:
No shadow falls beyond his reach, no tear is cried in vain.
Chorus
Because I set my love on him, he lifts me from the deep,
He answers when I call his name; he holds me while I weep.
In trouble, he will be my strength, my refuge, and my light,
With long and lingering years ahead, he comforts me each night.

The sunrise cracks the darkened sky and terrors slip away,
And though the ache still lingers on, it softens as I pray.
The wounds I wear may never fade, yet mercy covers all,
For even in the lowest place, I'm sheltered when I fall.

Bridge
A thousand fears rise like a flood, but none shall swallow me,
For underneath his mighty wings, my soul is safe and free.

Chorus and Outro
The night still falls, but now I know it never falls alone,
For in the shadow of his love I walk; my grief is known.

PSALM 92: SONG OF THE REDEEMED

I've watched the dawn ignite the sky and bathe the earth in gold.
I've heard the rivers hum their tunes, their chattering in the cold.
Seen autumn trees explode with depth, the wheat fields dance with joy,
Experienced warmth and love and things no sorrow can destroy.

But nothing in this wondrous world, no matter where I go,
Can ever be compared with you for from you beauty flows.
Your steadfast faithfulness each night, your love each day reborn.
Your depth of thought exceeds my own, your works eclipse the dawn.

Chorus
And so, its good to give you thanks, sing praises and rejoice.
Declare your might with instruments of music, song, and voice.
Because the splendor of the world reflects your grand design,
We worship you, our God and King, ineffably sublime.

My chains are dust, my debts are gone, my slate has been wiped clean.
The voice that once accused my soul, the sins that once would scream,
Have publicly been washed away and nailed up on that cross,
The powers of eternal night, their might disarmed and crushed.

You make me grow like tall palm trees, producing fruit all year,
I flourish in your presence, Lord, in you no longer fear.
From age to age you're still the same, O Lord, you do not change.
You won't forsake until the day my mortal frame's exchanged.

Chorus

Also based on Colossians 2:13–15.

PSALM 93: THE LORD REIGNS

Intro
The universe is firmly set and cannot be shaken.
Your throne is fixed and permanent and cannot be challenged, you are from everlasting . . .

I see them standing where the tide gnaws at the dunes, where the salt wind
Turns every stone to parchment. They lift their eyes to the unbowed hills,
To the sky where no hand has set a boundary. They murmur words
That outlive the years, though none will carve them in marble.

Chorus
Your statutes stand, O Lord, secure, more sure than time, more pure than light.
Holiness crowns your house forever, your throne unshaken in the flood.

The rivers rise, they say, the waves hurl their weight against the shore,
But still he reigns. Before the first stone turned in the depths, before
The sun spilled gold upon the sea, his throne endured. And still they stand,
Unnamed, unnoted, bearing witness to the rock beneath the flood.

Outro
The universe is firmly set and cannot be shaken.
Your throne is fixed and permanent and cannot be challenged, you are from everlasting . . .

PSALM 94: HE WHO MADE THE EAR AND EYE

I watch them rise and see their deeds and hear their mocking words.
They crush the poor, oppress the weak, the lines of justice blurred.
O God of vengeance, God of truth, how long will you be still?
Arise, O Judge of all the earth and let us know your will.

Pre-Chorus
Although they think that they are wise, yet they lack understanding;
The logic's inescapable and fully reprimanding.
Chorus
Shall he who made the earth and sky and hung the moon and stars,
Or he who set the boundaries of seas and lands enlarged,
Shall he who made the ear and eye not hear or shan't he see?
The source of wisdom and of truth, shall he not set decrees?

Perhaps the wicked, senseless ones will never hear the Lord,
But we who claim to follow him, and know his living Word,
Must see in our adversity the lessons to be learned;
As time will show that, in his grace, they shall be overturned.

Pre-Chorus and Chorus

Yes, we may see the wicked rise, but we will see them fall.
The things that may assault our faith and press us to the wall,
May be the opportunity for God to show his might,
In justice and in righteousness, he will put all things right.

Pre-Chorus, Chorus, and Outro
The thoughts of fools are but a breath and though they stand like trees,
They cannot last for God will make them fall like autumn leaves.

PSALM 95: THE ROCK OF AGES CALLS MY NAME

I stand before you, King of kings, and sing my song of praise,
O sovereign Lord, I stand in awe and worship you always.
The mountain heights and ocean depths are in your mighty hand.
The sky, the land, the universe, all subject to your plan.

The ground on which we walk is yours, the planets and the sun,
You, in your grace, selected us to be your chosen ones,
You're our Creator, Mediator, Savior, and Friend,
And so we sing and so we praise the one we comprehend.

Chorus
So, brother, sister, come and sing, come and bow before him.
He is the rock of our salvation; he's the King of kings.
We do not sing in empty space, but we sing face-to-face,
For in your presence there is joy and overflowing grace.

Dear Lord, we want to worship you, please help us with our lives,
For we believe and we do trust that in your Word we'll thrive,
And once you have begun the work, you'll bring it to completion,
That we may enter your great rest in every generation.

Bridge
Take up the music instruments and make a happy song,
Let's lift our voices, shout for joy, and praise and sing as one.
O come let's worship, come bow down and kneel before our Maker,
For he's our God and we're his sheep, and he is our Redeemer.

Chorus and Outro
I stand before you, King of kings, and sing my song of praise.
O sovereign Lord, I stand in awe and worship you always.

PSALM 96: WORSHIP HIM, YOUR ONE TRUE GOD

With heart and mind I will compose a new song to you, Lord.
With instruments and melody I'll write harmonious chords.
I'll tell of your deliverance from slavery and sin
And bless you with my heart and soul as every day begins.

O nations, hear the truth proclaimed, the Lord alone is King.
And he is greater than the gods and other worthless things.
His handiwork and majesty no one can ascertain,
His splendor and omnipotence no one can quite explain.

Chorus
Ascribe to God from age to age the glory due his name.
The brilliance of his holiness and greatness of his fame.
Present to him your mortal selves a living sacrifice
And worship him, your one true God, who is the Lord of light.

He is Creator of all things; through him all things exist.
By power of his holy Word, in him all things persist.
O let the universe be glad, and let the earth rejoice,
Let oceans roar, the fields exult, the forests sing for joy.

He comes with mercy, robed in light, to set the world to rights.
No sword of greed, no throne of lies, can stand before his sight.
In justice and in righteousness he will be Judge of all,
And human ideologies will crumble and will fall.

Chorus

Also based on Romans 12:1; Hebrews 1:3.

PSALM 97: YOUR AIM IS STILL TO BLESS

Intro
You, O Lord, are good and great, a God of certainty,
And so we praise, our voices raise in grateful harmony.

The storm approached with swirling clouds as lightning tore the sky;
The thunder shook the mountain tops, the wind howled in reply.
The foaming waves struck at the coast as darkness veiled the moon,
And every creature small and great in terror scurried home.

Chorus
Above the things that bring us pain and cause us great distress,
You still are weaving all for good, your aim is yet to bless.

Above the fire in the night, the one who rules and reigns
Is firmly seated on his throne and he alone restrains
Destructive forces and commands the great angelic bands,
And he preserves the lives of all who dwell within his hands.

Chorus

For you, O Lord, are far above the heavens and the earth,
You are exalted way beyond the furthest universe.
A righteous and compassionate deliverer divine,
A mighty King who still directs the world he has designed.

Outro
Yes, we rejoice for you are good, a God of certainty,
And so we praise, our voices raise in grateful harmony.

PSALM 98: A SONG NEWLY COMPOSED

Intro
We sing to you, our Lord and King, a song newly composed,
For you are great and marvellous, and from you mercy flows.

The songs of your redeeming grace cannot be secondhand,
They must come fresh from every breast and from there should expand.
For each successive day you come to meet us all again,
Your mercies new, your faithfulness and kindness never end.

Chorus
And so, with joy, we come once more to voice our thankful praise
With gladsome noise and melodies and reconstructed phrase.
Our hearts renewed for we have viewed your great deliverance,
As at the cross you have revealed divine benevolence.

We see your great and glorious, creative grand design,
All infinite in variation, perfectly defined.
The roaring ocean and the seas and all that lives in them,
The earth with its complexities, the stars, the moon, the sun.

Chorus

But grander still beyond the world and all we can discuss,
The new creation demonstrates the love you have for us.
And, looming large for all to see, an untenanted cross,
Salvation has been finalized at your expense and cost.

Chorus and Outro
We sing to you, our Lord and King, a song newly composed,
For you are great and marvellous, and from you mercy flows.

PSALM 99: WE WORSHIP YOU, LORD GOD ALMIGHTY

The hush as I enter your presence, your majesty comes into view,
The quietness, just like a staircase, inevitably leads me to you.
You're higher than the highest heavens, you're purer than all mountain brooks,
More radiant than dozens of diamonds, and wiser than millions of books.

Chorus
We worship you, Lord God Almighty! For you are our majestic King.
You're holy, you're wise, and you're loving, you're timeless in your sovereignty.

You silence a storm with a whisper, you heal us with barely a word.
All evil will flee from your presence, resistance is rendered absurd.
For you are a King who loves justice, and truth is your very desire.
You're righteous, yet always forgiving, and mercy is what you require.

Chorus

PSALM 100: OUR SHEPHERD KING

With instruments of music and with our songs of praise
    we make a joyful melody, in harmony we raise
Our voices and our grateful hearts to you, our Shepherd King,
    and of your great deliverance, in thankfulness, we sing.

Chorus
For you have opened up the gate that we may enter in.
    Good Shepherd you laid down your life, defeated death and sin.
You tore the separating veil and we stand in your courts,
    we are your flock for, with your blood, each one of us was bought.

You are the one who spoke and everything we know began,
    but sin had blocked our way to you; yet now, by your command,
In Jesus we are re-created, raised to live with you,
    and we are held in nail-pierced hands in which we are renewed.

Chorus

We sing to you, our risen Lord, for you alone are good,
    your steadfast love and faithfulness shown on a cross of wood.
Through you we have eternal life, for death has lost its sting,
    and so, as yours forevermore, we'll serve you, Shepherd King.

Chorus

PSALM 101: RIGHT CHOICES

O Lord, as you are well aware, my character is flawed
    because of sin and selfishness, I often am a fraud,
For I display a godliness for all the world to see
    while in my heart, perverse and stark, I am concerned with me.

Chorus
So, I will sing of righteousness, of mercy, and of love,
    of justice and of faithfulness, of truth and grace above.
I'll set my heart to follow you, to walk within your ways,
    to honor you in all I do for all my living days.

And so, I must begin with self and bring your will to bear
    upon my conduct and my life that I may even dare
To demonstrate integrity, to wisely walk the path
    that leads me ever closer to the life for which I'm tasked.

Chorus

I am determined to obey and make your word my guide,
    and now I know I need your help; I need you by my side.
Without your presence leading me to honor and to serve,
    my private life will never change, nor will I be preserved.

Chorus

I also will surround myself with that which will uphold
    your justice and your dignity, to bring under control
Whatever seeks to overthrow your good and perfect law;
    morality is easily changed when goodness is withdrawn.

Chorus

PSALM 102: THE YEARS MAY PASS

O Lord, I cry to you once more, please hear me when I call.
    My days, like smoke, are blown away, like whispers on the wind.
They vanish with the break of day and won't return at all.
    My pain consumes my appetite, O Lord, forgive my sin.

My heart is winnowed like the grass and withers as in drought.
    My bones are dry, my strength is dust, my tongue is parched with grief.
A lonely sparrow with no home, an owl that has no house,
    my youth has gone, my yesterdays fade like the autumn leaves.

My bread is ash, my tears are drink, my skin clings to my frame.
    I fade, yet still, O Lord, you shine, unchanged through years of shame.
I watch my colleagues dim with time, their faces turn to shade.
    The echoes of my childhood life are lost where shadows fade.

Chorus
But you, O Lord, are on your throne, your kingdom cannot fall.
    Enthroned throughout eternity, a King for great and small.
The years may pass, the winds may groan, but you are Lord of all.

Like shadows in the evening sun that slowly fade from view,
    my life hangs in the balance as time keeps slipping through
The fingers of my aging hands; and yet, you are the one
    who hears the groans of all the generations yet to come.

I may be dust upon the ground, a reed upon the shore,
    but you're the one who lifts my soul so I may dwell secure.
And though the earth may wilt and wane, and though the sky may fade,
    you will remain the holy one, I need not be afraid.

Chorus

PSALM 103: THE MYSTERY OF HIS SOVEREIGNTY, THE MIRACLE OF GRACE

O my soul, lift up your voice and bless the Lord of light,
Who heals the wounds of sin and shame and lifts the lost to life.
The dust of all our graceless years he scatters to the wind,
His mercy like an ocean tide that pulls us back again.

I searched and prayed for insight to the heart of God's design,
And found a love and grace so vast that I could not define
What seems incomprehensible; no poet can compose
Nor can describe a goodness that is more than we suppose.

Chorus
So, from my inner depths I will exalt his holy name,
For he is great and marvellous, his faithfulness remains.
He satisfies my hungry heart and gives me what is best;
On eagle's wings he lifts me up and crowns me with his rest.

In righteousness and equity he fights for the oppressed,
Removing our iniquity as far as east from west,
He knows that we are weak and frail, remembers we are dust,
And so he is compassionate to everyone who trusts.

The mystery of his sovereignty, the miracle of grace,
A love unshaken through the years, a pledge that will not break.
And though our days are like the grass that grows yet soon is gone,
The steadfast love of God remains, and in him we are strong.

Chorus

PSALM 104: MAY MY CONTEMPLATION BE A PLEASING THING TO HIM

He bathes the day in golden fire, the dawn is washed with flame,
The heavens arch, a boundless dome, the sky a sweet refrain.
With whispers on the perfumed breeze, the folded clouds are built,
They spill their treasure on the land and thirsty fields are filled.

The rivers carve the sleeping plains, the valleys drink their streams,
The trees are heavy, drenched in green, their sighing speaks of dreams.
And in their branches high above, the birds sing symphonies,
The grass and plants are food for all, the earth is satisfied.

Chorus
So, may the glory of the Lord endure forevermore.
For he is clothed in majesty, in light, and in splendor.
I'll sing to him while I have breath, while I still have my being,
And may my contemplation be a pleasing thing to him.

The mountain goats leap peak to peak, the badgers hide in caves,
The planets measure time and space, the seasons are engraved.
The lions prowl beneath the moon, they seek their food at night,
But when the sun ignites the sky, they vanish out of sight.

The sea unfurls its endless roar, the waves build up and crash,
The teeming fish, in laughing swells, explode in silvery flash.
And every creature lives and breathes exactly as God wills,
For everyone upon the earth is subject to him still.

Chorus

He sends his breath; the dust revives, the lifeless stand and dance,
The grass erupts in verdant green, the meadows wave and prance.
But should he turn his face away, the world would halt and die,
As ashes claim the grieving heart, the empty spirit cries.

Yet still I sing, while breath remains, while stars are set alight,
While oceans churn and forests rise, and shadows birth the night.
But when my song's no longer heard, my flesh interred in clay,
Let echoes of his mighty name outlive my fleeting day.

Chorus

PSALM 105: THE PRIORITY AND PERSEVERANCE OF GOD'S AMAZING GRACE

O sing, give thanks, and call upon his holy, mighty name!
Tell of his wonders to the world; let every voice proclaim!
For he has chosen, not for worth, nor strength, nor human will,
But by his love alone he called and calls his people still.

He made a covenant of grace, unshaken through all time,
A promise bound by steadfast love, unbroken by our crimes.
Before one law was set in stone, he bought us as his own,
Delivered first, then sanctified, built on the Cornerstone.

When famine fell upon the land, when hunger turned to grief,
He raised up Joseph from the pit to be their sure relief.
Through shackled years and darkened cells, his dreams at last came true.
God's hidden hand was working still, his mercy always new.

But Israel came to slavery, a stranger in restraints,
Yet God increased them mightily and heard their loud complaints.
And Pharaoh's heart grew hard with hate, his deviousness increased,
God's mercy moved to intervene as Pharaoh overreached.

He sent the plagues, he tore the sky with thunderous fire and hail,
He darkened days, he shattered pride, and over gods prevailed.
Then with a mighty outstretched arm, he set his people free,
Not by their strength, nor by their might, but by his own decree.

Through parted waves, through desert wastes, his pillar led them on,
He fed them bread, provided drink under that desert sun.
Still law would come from Sinai's heights, but grace is first and last,
And not for merit, not for deed, but his unchanging heart.

They wandered far, they turned away, at times misunderstood,
Yet though they failed a thousand times, his covenant still stood.
He led by nothing else but love, he spoke, and it was done,
The grace that chose would persevere until the race was won.

So, let the nations hear his name, let every tongue recall,
Not first the law, not first the call, but mercy over all.
For grace is God's priority, beginning and the end,
His love remains far deeper than all we comprehend.

PSALM 106: REMEMBER ME

My life hangs in the balance as I read through your word,
    bad choices, empty promises have made life seem absurd.
But as I read, I understand that others in the past
    rejected you, yet in their need, they turned to you at last.

Your people, when in Egypt, cast aside the one you sent,
    and even when you led them out through many great events,
They soon forgot and made a calf to worship that instead,
    and many other times they sinned, when they were all misled.

Chorus
O Jesus, please remember me as you are on your throne,
    and save me in your graciousness, so I am not alone.
Cause me to hear those wondrous words you spoke upon the cross,
    "In paradise you'll be with me, and you will not be lost."

And even when you led them to your precious promised land,
    they feared the giants and had no faith in your almighty hand.
They murmured in the wilderness of hunger and of thirst,
    repeatedly they angered you and many were dispersed.

They scorned the good land that you gave, and learned new wicked ways,
    they sacrificed their children to the demons on the plains.
And even after discipline by enemies around,
    they failed to serve you righteously, and so, they all were bound.

Chorus

But like them we have traded truth for falsehood and for lies,
    and in our wars the blood of children cries up to the skies.
For in our own enlightenment, we do what is not wise,
    and in our thoughtlessness, we see that finally right dies.

Yet you will still remember me, your mercy stays the same,
    for every soul who turns to you and calls upon your name.
So, in the darkness of my doubts and in my deepest fears
    I know that you are with me still, through all my living years.

Chorus

Also based on Luke 23:42–43.

BOOK FIVE

Psalms 107–150

PSALM 107: OUR GRACIOUS, FORGIVING DELIVERER

As I linger in the spaces of your absence in my need,
    and I hunger for the laughter we once shared abundantly,
I let the echoes of your presence fill the emptiness inside,
    and once more I am reminded, even scars reflect your light.

And at times I sit in darkness, thorns of anger in my chest,
    for the words that you have spoken were not hidden in my breast.
I rebelled and spurned the counsel of your wise and holy law,
    yet I know that you will hear me when I pray to you once more.

Chorus
For you're gracious and forgiving and you satisfy my soul,
    as you shatter bars of iron, make my ruined pieces whole.
You deliver from destruction, still my storms and hush the waves,
    turn my deserts into rivers, as you lift me from my grave.

When I'm stricken with afflictions caused by vain and foolish ways,
    when the oceans of my memory toss me back and forth again.
When I'm reeling like a drunkard that has drained the vats of hell,
    still, I know that you are wondrous and you free me from my cell.

When diminished by oppression, and reduced to tears and pain,
    even those you place above me are controlled and are constrained.
For you pour contempt on tyrants as you raise the weak and the poor,
    and you silence all that's evil, breaking through its prison doors.

Chorus

PSALM 108: WITH YOU WE WILL DO VALIANTLY

The morning sun sings softly through the curtains of my room,
    of things I take for granted and of things I have assumed.
Your steadfast love and faithfulness immeasurable at best,
    are greater than I ever will be able to express.

So, be exalted, O my God, above the highest heights
    your glory shines throughout the earth as you set things to rights.
Deliver all your children, keep the promises you made,
    for God, if you've rejected us then how shall we be saved?

O grant us help against the one who seeks to do us harm
    for we are weak and powerless, yet I am not alarmed.
With you we will do valiantly, you will tread down our foes,
    and I will sing a melody and praise songs I'll compose.

PSALM 109: CONFRONTING EVIL WITH PRAYER

A sulphurous smog slinks to my door and fingers for a key,
    it seeks for entrance through the mouths of those who threaten me.
With silver tongues and lying hearts, they circle me like prey,
    and violently, without a cause, they close in to betray.

Responding to my love with hate, they claim and they accuse,
    what can I do but bend my knees and turn in prayer to you?
Rewarding me with wrong for right, they seek my bitter end,
    do not be silent, O my God, I call for your defense.

Confront the wicked ones that seek destruction of the weak,
    bring judgment on the charlatans and all their foul techniques.
The ground that drank the blood they spilled pleads justice and revenge,
    reverse the curse that they invoke, let truth itself avenge.

May hollow plots recoil on those who fashion guile and greed,
    may those who prey upon the poor yet feel as those they bleed.
May all judicial systems hold, let none succumb to bribes,
    may nests of snakes not use their stealth or wealth to override.

Let schemers reap the seeds they've sown, let false accusers fall,
    let those who shunned the orphan's cry find none to heed their call.
Let mercy flee from hearts that scorned the wounded and the weak,
    let justice answer every lie, let truth unmask deceit.

May all they stole dissolve like mist, their names fade like the dust,
    their lamp be quenched, their house undone, for nothing built on lust
can stand before the Judge of all, whose throne is built on right;
    uncoil your whip and overrun the brigands and their might.

But as for me, O Lord my God, my refuge and my strength,
> your steadfast love will lift my soul, bring recompense at length.
Though they may curse, yet you will bless, the righteous will rejoice,
> salvation clothes the contrite heart that hearkens to your voice.

I praise the name of God Most High, whose mercy never fails,
> whose hand upholds the fainting heart, whose justice will prevail.
The needy shall not be ignored, the poor shall not be spurned,
> the righteous shall exult in him, for truth will not be burned!

PSALM 110: THE SCEPTER AND THE THRONE

The daylight spilled like silver on the thrones around the room,
    the twenty-four were clothed in garments light as sweet perfume,
And seated on a platform raised a step above the rest,
    the Lamb of God shone radiantly like jasper in the west.

I stood in awe in that great hall not knowing what to do,
    the rumbling of the thunder as the flames came into view,
The living creatures see all things in front and from behind
    their ceaseless chants of worship with the praise of all combined.

A scepter forged in sacrifice extended from his hand,
    its iron spine with gilded edge was stretched out on the land.
For he must reign until all evil things are on the floor,
    in the order of Melchizedek, he's priest forevermore.

The rivers rise, the mountains shake as war convulses lands,
    yet seated high, the sovereign Lord holds justice in his hand.
He calls his chosen witnesses, they answer in his might,
    arrayed in resurrection robes, they stride into the fight.

The cup of wrath, filled to the brim, the winepress stains the strand,
    a crimson flood that marks the march of heaven's dread command.
He lifts his head beside the stream, the battle at its close,
    the throne endures, the King prevails, and none will dare oppose.

Also based on Ezekiel 37:1–14; Revelation 4; 19.

PSALM 111: HIS PRAISE ENDURES ALWAYS

All my heart will sing his praise among the gathered throng,
    Boundless are his works of might, enduring firm and strong.
Clothing all his deeds with grandeur, justice marks his ways,
    Day by day his mercy shines in faithful love and grace.

Evermore his wonders stand, remembered through the years,
    Feeding those who trust in him, dispelling all their fears.
Gracious is the Lord of hosts, his covenant secure,
    Hope is found in all his words; unchanging, true, and pure.

In his hands are strength and power; his precepts guide the soul,
    Joyful are the ones who see his promises unfold.
Kings may rise and rulers fall, but still his name remains,
    Lifting up the lowly ones, restoring what had waned.

Mighty are his hands that shape the heavens and the earth,
    Nations see his justice shine, declaring all his worth.
On his word the faithful stand, unshaken through the night,
    Promises he made endure; his truth is life and light.

Questions rise, yet wisdom waits for those who seek his face,
    Righteous are his works, adorned with mercy, love, and grace.
Steady is his guiding hand, his ways are tried and true,
    Those who fear the Lord will find his steadfast Word renews.

Unknown depths of holy awe belong to those who trust,
    Voices lift his name on high, his judgments pure and just.
Wonders, vast beyond our grasp, reveal his heart and will,
    Xenith of all wisdom; those who love him seek him still.

Years will pass, but he remains, the Lord, our rock, our praise,
Zeal and awe shall crown his name forever and always.

Based on Psalm 111, using the same acrostic style.

PSALM 112: REFLECTIONS

In deep introspection I ponder the question of where I belong.
    For no rhyme or reason, I am in this season of muddling along.
I sit and I ponder, and then as I wonder, I think of the moon.
    It is a reflection, a mere recollection, of light from the sun.

And so, in my thinking, I find myself linking this fact to my life,
    for what I am showing is not of my knowing but mirrors his light.
The grace that remakes me, that holds me and shapes me, is not of my hand,
    and yet in his favour, I find that my labour is blessed and expands.

God's children who follow will shine through tomorrow with stars in their wake,
    their love is unshaken, their hope is not taken, their vows do not break.
Their home is a haven, a nourishing station where all may find peace,
    a shelter from sorrow, for even the sparrow, where mercies increase.

Compassion flows freely, they give to the needy with hands open wide,
    their judgment is steady, their hearts ever ready with God as their guide.
They lend without measure, and yet they will treasure the trust they have earned,
    their steps never wander but always grow stronger in truth they have learned.

No shadow can shake them, no slander unmake them, they walk without fear,
    in every misfortune, they act in proportion, because God is near.
Though tempests may thunder, and tear hope asunder, their trust will remain,
    for light everlasting will soon be surpassing the darkness reclaimed.

The wicked behold them, unreasonably curse them, but still they endure,
    for joy built on malice from a bitter chalice can never be sure.
Yet those who are righteous will shine in his brightness and never be moved,
    for all they inherit is drawn from the credit of what Jesus has proved.

For he's our example, comparative sample, of infinite grace,
    he feared and he followed, he knelt in the hollow and lifted his face.
For in sacrificing, he was demonstrating the love he displays,
    and all who receive him, reflect and believe him, will walk in his ways.

So, let us not falter, but stand at the altar of mercy for then,
    though dust is our making, his glory is taking its shape once again.
The moon in its brightness is not in the slightest as bright as the sun,
    and yet, in our gleaming, his radiance is streaming, and his will is done.

PSALM 113: I'LL SING THE NAME OF JESUS CHRIST

The darkness was so deep that I could not tell truth from lies,
    not even when reality was right before my eyes.
Dazed, confused, disoriented, I stood on unseen ground.
    Unsure of where I truly was or what might lurk around.

The only sense of up or down was felt beneath my feet.
    If numbness took that anchor, too, I'd have to face retreat.
I raised my hands and gingerly, with my fingers far outstretched,
    I shuffled forward cautiously, for fear of sore regret.

Then slowly through the curtain cracks, the light began to dawn,
    and as the shadows ceased to be, I knew my fears were gone.
For though I may not know what lies in store for me this day,
    I know my God is with me every step along the way.

He is the one who lifts the poor and weary from the dust.
    He will not leave the needy on the ashen heaps to rust.
He raises them and causes them to sit on royal thrones,
    and he's the one who saves and gives the barren women homes.

So, I will bless the living Lord whose name is high above
    all powers and dominions—yet I know his name is love.
From dawn to dusk, from dusk to dawn, from east and to the west,
    I'll sing the name of Jesus Christ, for he is to be blessed.

PSALM 114: THE SONG OF THE EXODUS

When Israel fled from slavery, the Lord went on before,
    the house of Jacob bolted from the lash of Pharaoh's roar.
The sea saw God and turned in fear, the Jordan shrank away,
    the hills leapt high like startled rams, the mountains shook and swayed.

What bothers you, that you should flee? And Jordan, why retreat?
    Why dance, you hills, like skipping lambs, and mountains on your feet?
Earth, tremble at the presence of the God who split the sea,
    who turned the flint to fountains, with his waters flowing free.

But more than dust and water moved one night beneath the stars,
    the powers of hell were shaken by the Lamb who bore our scars.
Our Red Sea parted from the tomb, our chains fell in the tide,
    and Jordan split from north to south, the day our Savior died.

And Satan fell, his gates were breached, his darkness crushed and drowned.
    The Jordan's final flood was tamed when Christ rose from the ground.
Now saints arise, a pilgrim throng, and march into the fight,
    our cloud by day, our fire by night, the Lord our guiding light.

The exodus was just the view; fulfilment was the cross
    where Jesus paid our penalty so we would not be lost.
The heart of stone now gushes grace, the barren soul finds spring,
    and heaven's angels leap for joy to hear the ransomed sing.

PSALM 115: OUR LIVING GOD

I stood before the monolithic idol in the room,
    its features carved in marble clothed in elegant costume.
What made the ancient fathers think that this mute block of stone
    could rescue them in times of need and hear them when they groaned?

They do have mouths but cannot speak, and ears but cannot hear,
    nor can they see into our souls nor take away our fears.
And though they have the attributes of every living thing,
    they'll always be inanimate, like puppets on a string.

And yet we have a substitute that takes on many forms,
    the things we cannot live without, the tangible transformed.
It may be stocks it may be shares, or lives of greed and ease,
    but things that have no heart or soul that cannot offer peace.

Although we may have changed the form, the idols stay the same,
    they are the work of human hands and cannot ease the strain
Of sin and death and disconnect between us and our God,
    for ultimately all they are, are things made out of gold.

But there is one who speaks and sees and closely is involved
    with every aspect of our lives and all round him revolves.
He is our help, he is our shield, in him we place our trust,
    the one who made the earth and sky will never be unjust.

So, not to us, no, not to us, but to your name be praise,
    your steadfast love and faithfulness leads us through all our days.
You bless us all, both great and small, and through you we increase,
    so, we will bless our living God in whom we have our peace.

PSALM 116: I LOVE THE LORD

In depths of darkness, I descended to the very brink of hell,
    the consequence of hope deferred was so unparalleled
        that nothing could alleviate my pain and my distress,
    until I called upon the Lord to save me from this mess.

He knew I mocked him, yet he still reached out to me in love,
    for even though I needed him, I could not look above
        the highest wall I'd built around my fragile inner self,
    and still he heard unspoken prayers and took me to himself.

I love the Lord for he has heard my silent cries for aid,
    and though the snares of sin and death had made me so afraid,
        he rescued me and carried me till I could walk with him,
    he dried my tears and set me back upon my feet again.

What shall I render to my Lord for all his benefits?
    I'll celebrate his victory and praise his selflessness.
        I will fulfil my promises and give my all to him
    and as his servant I will serve him as my God and King.

PSALM 117: OUR GRACIOUS GOD

It never ceases to amaze how we, who are for grace,
    are always quick to criticise our Lord straight to his face.
And even though we know that we are nothing on our own,
    we find the splinter in the eye of those we will disown.

Why can't we see that great is he who's faithful to the end?
    His steadfast love's immeasurable, on that we can depend.
So, why find fault when all about we see his patient hand
    that leads his stubborn people on into his promised land.

How dare we point the finger at another saved by grace,
    while we are teaching others that we cannot merit faith?
Instead, we should be praising him that he does not treat us
    the way we treat each other, throwing them under the bus.

And like the Pharisees of old, we smugly claim that we
    are justified in what we say, and so we all agree.
And all the time our Savior weeps for those we sweep aside;
    "My child," he says, "do you not know, it's them for whom I died?"

So, let us rather praise and sing to him who graciously
    did all that needed to be done to set us captives free.
And surely once our eyes are firmly set upon the cross,
    we'll see that all we once thought gain should really count as loss.

PSALM 118: THE LOVE THAT BEARS US ENDLESSLY

It felt like I'd been cornered in the darkness of my soul,
    and life became an onslaught as I seemed to lose control,
With fingers of dejection tightly grasping at my throat,
    depleting all my energy to merely stay afloat.

But then in my despondency I cried out to my Lord,
    repeating all the promises contained within his word.
Not only did he answer me, he also set me free,
    and so I overcame the things that were attacking me.

And through the burning wreckage of my complicated life,
    the truth came like a sudden flood and took me by surprise:
If God is truly on my side, then why am I afraid
    when dreadful things explode on me like deadly hand grenades?

Though earth begins to tremble, and my sky falls down in grief,
    and every step I try to take is fraught with disbelief,
When scaffolds of my certainty are cracking at the seams,
    the ground beneath me tilting like the landscape of my dreams,

Then still, beneath this wreckage, I hear a distant chord,
    a whisper, in the whirlwind, of the kindness of my Lord.
It calls me through the silence with a voice both fierce and kind:
    "My love endures forever; leave your fear and dread behind."

I stumble through the aftermath where nothing feels intact,
    where memories grow heavier, and thoughts refuse to act.
The world becomes a corridor of doors that will not budge,
    and every voice inside me turns to cynic, priest, and judge.

But even in that chamber where my sorrow multiplies,
    a crack appears—so narrow that it's hard to classify.
Yet through that fragile fracture shines a light I can't explain:
    a warmth that does not promise ease but stands with me in pain.

I found a gate flung open in the middle of my night,
    not guarded by illusion but by undeserving light.
He welcomes weary travellers with scars they cannot hide,
    and beckons all to enter in to love personified.

And there—a stone the builders spurned, now anchoring the whole,
    the axis of our suffering, the refuge of the soul.
He stands where all our chaos meets a greater, gracious plan:
    the Love that bears us endlessly, now meets us as a Man.

PSALM 119: YOUR WORD, MY WAY

Aleph
Blessed are those whose walk is pure and whole,
Who seek the Lord with an unblemished heart,
And keep his ways as purpose, path, and goal.

From his commandments they do not depart,
His laws and precepts direct all their ways,
And from his Word they will not drift or part.

You laid down your teachings for all our days
That we might keep them with a steadfast will,
To meditate and follow in your ways.

O may I not be reckoned void or still,
May my activities set me apart
And shape my restless thoughts to match your will.

Then I will praise you with a moral heart,
Upright, rejoicing in your Word's delight.
O please do not leave me; never depart.

Beth
O please do not leave me; never depart.
For how can the young stay pure in the way?
By keeping your Word right from the start.

With my whole heart I seek you every day,
Let me not wander from your wise command,
Let your Word be the lamp that lights my way.

Your Word is burned within me as a brand,
That I might not sin or forget your grace.
Your truth alone can help me where I stand.

Blessed are you, O Lord, in every place!
Teach me your statutes, write them on my tongue,
Let all your judgments shine before my face.

With my lips I declare all your commands,
I delight in your Word more than in gold,
And I will not forget all your demands.

Gimel
And I will not forget all your demands.
For pilgrims on this earth are not alone,
If your Word is not concealed but expands.

Open my eyes to see what you have shown,
The wonders hidden in your sacred law,
I am spent with longing for what's unknown.

A stranger here, yet filled with holy awe,
Your statutes are the compass of my soul,
Surer than earth's imagined lure or law.

My soul yearns with desires manifold
For all your decrees, constant, true, and just.
Though leaders scorn, I cling to what's been told.

Your Word is my delight, my shield, my trust.
I keep it close when others do me wrong,
Its wisdom lifts my head up from the dust.

Daleth
Its wisdom lifts my head up from the dust.
Revive me, Lord, according to your Word,
For in my grief, I've placed you in my trust.

I laid my ways before you and was heard,
You taught me how to walk in what is right,
A trembling soul upheld by what I've learned.

Help me to cling to you with all my might.
Remove deceit, make mercy my defense,
And let your path be ever my delight.

I choose the way of truth, not of pretense,
Your judgments laid before me clear and wide;
O let me never be filled with suspense.

I do not lag or falter, flee, or hide,
My heart expands when held within your hand,
For you have drawn me ever to your side.

He
For you have drawn me ever to your side;
Now teach me, Lord, the pathway of your will,
That in your statutes I may still abide.

Give understanding; light my shadows still,
That I may keep your law with joy unstrained,
And walk your path with undivided will.

Incline my heart away from selfish gain,
And turn my eyes away from worthless schemes.
Preserve my life by what your words sustain.

Establish me in certainty, not dreams.
Fulfill the hope your promises provide,
Let not my dread outweigh what you redeem.

I long for you, for truth to be my guide,
Revive me in your holy truth applied,
And let no reproach take root nor preside.

Waw
And let no reproach take root nor preside.
Let steadfast love and mercy come to me,
The truth on which I rely and confide.

Then I will answer all those who taunt me,
For I have placed my hope in what you say,
A hope that will remain continually.

In keeping your Word I will never stray,
For in your judgments, I have set my course.
They are my song, my strength along the way.

I'll keep your law through time without remorse;
I walk in freedom, for I seek your will,
Not hindered by the proud or by their force.

Before all rulers my mouth shall be filled,
Your precepts are the joy my soul has known,
And in your love, I lift my hands up still.

Zayin
And in your love, I lift my hands up still,
Remembering the Word you gave to me.
A promise that sustains my heart and will.

This is my comfort in adversity:
Your Word revives me; though the proud deride,
Their scorn cannot disturb your truth in me.

I've kept your laws though darkness surged inside.
Your ancient rules have been my song and rest,
A steady chord that sorrow can't divide.

At night I sing them, and my soul is blessed.
I think upon your name and find my peace,
For what you have spoken I will profess.

This has become my own, your love's increase,
That I have kept your precepts, known and dear,
Through every storm, in exile or release.

Heth
Through every storm, in exile or release,
You are my portion, Lord; I've made my choice,
And in your presence my soul finds true peace.

With all my heart I've sought to hear your voice.
I walk in the testimonies you gave,
Repenting before guilt disturbs my choice.

Though cords of wicked men like snares enslave,
I'll not remove your law from mind or heart,
It is the hope through which I will be saved.

At midnight I'll arise and sing apart
Because all your ways and rules are so wise,
The motivating point from which I start.

All those who fear you, Lord, I recognize,
And I will walk with them through dark and light,
For the earth's filled with love before my eyes.

Teth
For the earth's filled with love before my eyes.
You've dealt with me according to your Word,
A kindness that affliction can't disguise.

Teach me good judgment, let my heart be stirred.
Before you broke me, I had gone astray,
But now I cling to all that I have heard.

You are so good, and you do good, the way
of mercy shaped my truth in tested flame,
You guide me still, though trials fill the day.

The brazen insult and slander my name,
But I will keep your precepts in my soul,
And let your fear refine my inward frame.

Their hearts are leaden, unfeeling and cold,
But I rejoice in pain that makes me whole;
Your Word is better than the finest gold.

Yodh
Your Word is better than the finest gold.
You formed my hands, and you will guide my path,
Your wisdom makes the weak and weary bold.

Give me understanding, Lord, and start
To teach my soul what you have called me to.
Your Word guards me as I your truth impart.

Though sinners seek to stray and lead me through
their paths of error, I will follow none,
As your commandments are forever true.

Let all who fear you see my life begun,
I seek your law and keep it night and day,
The work you've started, Lord, will be well done.

Let not the proud come near me to dismay,
But let my soul rejoice in every way,
And in your peace my heart will always stay.

Kaph
And in your peace my heart will always stay.
Though I am like a wineskin in the smoke,
Yet I've not forgotten to walk your way.

How long must your servant still be provoked
By those who persecute and hurt my soul?
They all have not believed the Word you spoke.

They seek to bring me under their control.
May your wisdom help me through all my days,
I keep your precepts and make them my goal.

They almost made an end of all my ways,
But I have kept your precepts, which I trust
To guide me and to lead me through the haze.

In your steadfast love may my steps adjust,
For I walk in your light as I am dust.
I keep your testimonies that I trust.

Lamedh
I keep your testimonies that I trust.
Forever Lord, your Word is firmly fixed,
Your faithfulness establishes the just.

For in your law my soul is quite transfixed,
A way for me to walk without regret,
It kept me safe through every sad conflict.

Your precepts, Lord, I simply won't forget,
For by them you have given me my life,
And I will be forever in your debt.

I know that at best we remain finite,
But your commandments are comprehensive
And so, they will always be my delight.

Mem
And so, they will always be my delight,
And in them I will meditate always.
They make me wiser than my foes at night.

I have more wisdom than those who appraise,
Because your Word is my meditation
I have more understanding than the aged.

I hold back my feet from what is brazen
That I might be submissive to your Word;
I will obey without hesitation.

And so, I will not compromise your Word,
For through it all I have been instructed,
All else is rendered totally absurd.

Your words are sweet, this I have deducted,
Therefore, I will renounce, and I reject
All the ways that others have constructed.

Nun
All the ways that others have constructed
Have no lantern to guide my weary feet;
By your Word my life has been adjusted.

I am severely afflicted by cheats,
Preserve my life according to your Word
And then I will forever be complete.

Accept my offerings of praises heard,
I hold my hands out continually,
I will not forget what I have preferred.

The wicked lay many snares to catch me
But I will never forsake your precepts,
Your testimonies are what keep me free.

They are my joy, what keeps my heart in check;
I dispose myself to do your statutes,
Forever they are what makes me perfect.

Samekh
Forever they are what makes me perfect.
That's why I hate all double-mindedness,
But I love and keep your holy precepts.

You are my hiding place and fortress,
So, my hope is in what you have revealed.
Depart from me all who do wickedness.

That I might keep the commandments received,
Uphold me according to your promise.
Let me not regret what I have believed.

Keep me that I may be safe and flawless
And have regard for your statutes always;
You disdain everyone who is lawless.

I will follow your Word all of my days
For I have a profound respect for you,
Your decrees guide me as I go and stay.

Ayin
Your decrees guide me as I go and stay.
So, as I have always done what is right,
Do not let my oppressors have their way.

Give your servant a pledge of what is right,
Do not let the insolent repress me;
Your promises are always in my sight.

O how I long for your saving decree.
According to your steadfast love and care,
Teach me to know all your testimonies.

It is time for you to act and to spare,
For your law has been trampled and broken.
Our faith as a nation has been impaired.

Therefore, I love all that you have spoken,
More than all diamonds and silver and gold.
May faith in you once more be awoken.

Pe
May faith in you once more be awoken.
Because your testimonies are wondrous,
Please reverse the gross global corrosion.

The recounting of your Word is glorious,
It grants comprehension to the simple,
In this your Word is always victorious.

Be gracious toward me lest I dwindle,
Please always keep me steady on my feet.
Always keep the flame of love rekindled.

Let no injustice lead to my defeat,
Redeem me from all forms of oppression,
May your protection always be complete.

Always hear my true and bold confession,
Make your face to shine upon your servant.
My eyes shed many tears of contrition.

Tsade
My eyes shed many tears of contrition.
But you are righteous and your rules are right,
In all faithfulness they have been written.

Because my enemies forget what's right,
My zeal for your holy Word consumes me,
It is the light that guides me through the night.

Your proven assurances hold the key
To everything that I consider dear,
For they have proved to be my certainty.

I'm inconsequential, scorned by my peers;
Yet I remember everything you say.
Your law is true despite their many sneers.

Your righteousness is righteous every day.
Though trouble and anguish have found me out,
Your commandments will keep me in the fray.

Qoph
Your commandments will keep me in the fray.
With my whole heart I cry to you, O Lord!
So, please do no let me be swept away.

Your testimonies are my sure reward,
And I will keep all your holy statutes.
I rise and cry for help before the dawn.

I meditate on all your attributes;
Awake I contemplate your promises
For your Word is final and absolute.

I believe that your justice harnesses
And keeps all evil purposes at bay,
So, I rest in your love and steadfastness.

You draw near to all those who know your way,
Who know that your commandments are true;
You gave them to us to help us each day.

Resh
You gave them to us to help us each day.
Please, deliver me from my affliction
And please do not let me be led astray.

For your laws are not like worldly fiction;
Give me life according to your promise,
As wickedness is the world's addiction.

Your mercy, O Lord, speaks for the speechless
For my adversaries are very loud.
I find their ideologies tasteless.

Ponder how I do not go with the crowd,
Consider how much I love your precepts.
And I do not do what is not allowed.

It is the truth of your Word I accept,
It is your steadfast love that gives me life.
Your eternal righteous rules are perfect.

Sin and Shin
Your eternal righteous rules are perfect.
Leaders persecute me without reason,
But my heart remains permanently set.

I rejoice in your Word every season
Like a person who has found great treasure;
So, I regard all falsehood as treason.

I praise you every day without measure
Because I love and keep your righteous rules;
And so, I will live in peace forever.

Your Word means more to me than many jewels.
Those who love your law will never stumble
And so they will not end their days as fools.

In following you I will not grumble,
For all my ways are ever before you;
Hence my life will never fail nor crumble.

Tav
Hence my life will never fail nor crumble.
Please give me understanding, O my Lord,
And deliver me for I am humble.

I make music and strike a joyful chord,
Because you train me in your precious Word;
Without you my whole life is flawed.

I have chosen to follow what I heard
In your teaching, in which is my delight.
In your sure salvation I am anchored.

For all your commandments are always right,
So, let your hand be ready to help me.
Let me run the race and fight the good fight.

O Lord, please seek your servant quickly
When I get lost and wander far away.
Guide and continue to lead me clearly.

Based on Psalm 119 according to the style of Guite, *David's Crown*.

PSALM 120: LYING LIPS

The viscous tongue lashed like a whip and slashed through my defense.
It groped with hooks of burning steel for things way too intense.
Those gentle lips that once spoke peace now curled up in a growl,
And suddenly the smiles of friends turned into ugly scowls.

What shall be done to narcissists who cannot see the harm
Of what they do to others who do not possess their charm
To influence the reticent or twist the minds of fools?
What shall be done? May God arise and speak to overrule.

Too long have I been silent here while sitting on a fence,
For when I speak the men of war eclipse all those with sense.
In my distress I called to you, O Lord, do not forget;
Deliver me from gossips who will simply not relent.

PSALM 121: MY PEACE IS FIRMLY FOUNDED

I stumbled through the garden gate, a message in my hand,
A burning flame of sorrow that I could not understand.
The air was thick with silence, like a hush before a cry,
And all the trees leaned in as if to hear me asking: "Why?"

My feet found gravel paths that led to hills I used to know,
I blundered on in anguish as I had nowhere to go.
I sought the calming presence of the silent natural world,
To calm my desolation where the torturous currents swirled.

There was no cry that could be heard, the pain was too intense,
And I was lost in stormy seas, the clouds were dark and dense.
My vision, blurred by salty tears, no longer could see light,
And suddenly, I'd reached an end with no more strength to fight.

I gazed upon the sleepy hills and wondered to myself,
To gain perspective in my trial, where could I turn for help?
And then I knew without a doubt my help comes from my Lord,
Creator of the earth and sky, and I'll not be ignored.

For though I cannot know what lies ahead for me right now,
The one who walks beside my path will carry me somehow.
And though I face a blazing sun or full-on harvest moon,
His presence will be with me like an autumnal perfume.

I cannot know what lies ahead in sickness, death, or health,
But this I know, my joy is not in worldly things nor wealth.
My going out and coming in is in far greater hands,
My peace is firmly founded on what we can't understand.

PSALM 121: HE HOLDS MY THEN, MY NOW, MY NEXT

My night is short, my nightmares tense, sleep seems beyond my reach.
I toss and turn like waves upon an endless stretch of beach.
The stars look on with silent eyes, and I feel small and frail,
A stranger set to sail again, I simply cannot fail.

My job is new, the stakes are high, the competition fierce.
They run a race I've just begun; my confidence is pierced.
As boxes pile behind the door, our lives are rearranged.
My children sleep not knowing yet how much their lives will change.

I think of friends and family, the ones I leave behind,
Of memories both good and bad, of those who've been unkind.
My mind is not a simple switch that can be forced to quit,
And as the clock keeps ticking on, emotions start to slip.

I stare into the ceiling's void, reciting all I know
Of promises and Scriptures that I learned so long ago.
And yet the stress still rises like hot lava in my throat:
O God, where is my help tonight? Why are you so remote?

Then like a gentle breeze that blows and cools a summer day,
The realization that you still are with me all the way
Releases all the waters that have dammed up deep inside:
The Lord who made the earth and sky will always be my guide.

He will not let my foot be moved, nor turn away his eyes,
Not one thing is unknown to him nor takes him by surprise.
So, if he is my keeper and the shade at my right hand,
The burning sun and freezing moon must bow to his command.

He safeguards every step I take, through every twist and turn,
And when I walk through foreign lands, the peace for which I yearn
Is not contingent on the circumstances that upend
The many things that he controls, on which I can depend.

So, as the sunlight lights the sky and I must face my day,
That peace that whispered in my night will not leave me dismayed.
My help comes from the Lord who stays when all my lights grow dim,
He holds my then, my now, my next and I am safe with him.

Dedicated to my brave eSwatini friend.

PSALM 122: MY PILGRIMAGE

The road was long and arduous, but I remember well
Elation at the prospect that totally dispelled
All thoughts of future weariness or dreariness ahead,
And all I saw were starry skies and sunny days instead.

The road lay like a ribbon, lengthy, silken threads of gold,
And though some nights were crystal clear, I did not mind the cold.
The landscapes that surrounded me, the freshness of the air,
The sweetness of the flowing fields, with birdsong everywhere.

But storm clouds gathered overhead, and rain began to fall,
And howling winds pushed back at me and slowed me to a crawl.
My feet sang a discordant tune, my muscles harmonized,
And dragging days and endless ways began to be despised.

And soon the pilgrimage became a battle to be won,
A struggle to be overcome, a taxing race to run.
And yet, in times of suffering, the darkness hummed with light,
And there I saw his table laid by cliffs of dolomite.

But with that final climb behind and standing on the crest,
God's city glowed before my eyes, as all the strain and stress
Of yesterday seemed faraway, as peace breathed like a hush,
And all my many doubts and fears embarrassingly blushed.

It's at this destination, where complexity and strife
Reveal in glorious tapestry the many threads of life,
It's here the sovereign architect, who paints in black and grey,
Unveils the many colors we had lost along the way.

PSALM 123: I WILL WAIT FOR RELEASE

I passed through silent hallways where not one had dared to speak,
A figure sat there waiting with a gaze serene and meek,
Were they waiting for a signal, a sign of unseen grace,
Neither anxious nor despairing, hope written on their face?

I was moved by their devotion, and I thought about my Lord,
Who has promised to be with us even when we feel ignored.
He has mercy on his people when they're held in sore contempt,
For from suffering and from anguish none of us can be exempt.

When my heartbeat is in spasms and my soul is tied in knots,
When the proud have moved against me with their foul and evil plots,
Like the figure in the hallway waiting patiently in peace,
I wait for you, my Father, for you will grant me release.

PSALM 124: WAVES OF ENDLESS MERCY

He could have killed me then and there, that would have been my end.
His anger was so fierce and sharp, no one could comprehend
The madness of his raging hate that swallowed me alive,
With bitterness and violence that took all by surprise.

His hands were tightly clasped, and they were closing round my neck,
My world began to swirl and whirl, my eyes saw dots and specks,
A flood began to sweep away my feet from off the floor,
But then the Savior of my soul came bursting through the door.

But in the major scheme of things, not one can have their way,
For even if they take my life, God has the final say.
My symphony of silence ends with thunderous timpani,
As waves of endless mercy all come singing over me.

Dedicated to the persecuted Church.

PSALM 125: UNCONQUERABLE

Relentless attacks showed no signs of abating,
Civilians and children were trapped in the quaking,
    Violently shaking
    church in which we were hiding
As women were crying and brave men were dying.

I lifted my head, and I looked down the aisle,
I had not frequented the church for a while,
But over the altar there hung from the rafters
A large crucifix that was made out of plaster.

Then softly within me, as faint as a whisper,
Came words once recited with brothers and sisters,
    Mothers and fathers
    in homes and in classrooms
That those who trust in the Lord shall never be moved.

For God will surround them, like mountains about them,
The scepter of wickedness shall surely be stemmed.
And all who are turned by their own crooked ways,
God will lead them away for he will not delay.

And though the explosions grew near, I was able,
By the words of the psalm, to believe I was stable,
    Unconquerable,
    as my soul lives on for ever,
As his Spirit is given to me without measure.

PSALM 126: FROM THE SHADOWS

The shattered shards of yesterday lay bleeding on the floor,
And any dreams and longings that I'd ever had before
Slid silently through holes and cracks that suddenly appeared,
And I knew then that I must face the things I'd come to fear.

My field of life, so barren now, was watered with my tears,
But leaden skies and burning heat and somber atmosphere
Had shriveled all my hopes for reaping seeds that I had sown,
And I surrendered to the fact that I was quite alone.

There was a time when laughter filled the air with peals of joy,
But like a flood my fortunes and my faith had been destroyed.
My weeping heart poured bitter wine into my empty soul,
And I despaired in agony of ever being whole.

But slowly in my misty mind the light began to break,
And from the shadows there arose as earth began to quake,
The very life I thought I'd lost that darkened day before,
As from the depths of death he rose as victor of the war.

PSALM 127: THE PROMISES OF TIME

The father came home late again, his children were in bed,
The mother worked a second job, she had no choice she said,
The children were too busy as their granny sat alone,
As many only theorize what makes a house a home.

They labour through the dead of night to spend what's not yet earned,
But anxious hands and sleepless minds forget what must be learned,
That if we build without the Lord, our labour is in vain,
Our hearts are thin, our lives cave in, and we're alone to blame.

Our screens glow bright, our voices fade, our meals are scoffed and gone.
We spend our time in solitude as days pass by in yawns.
No morals raised as hearts aren't trained, the Bible left unread,
And wisdom, an unwelcome guest, stands silently instead.

Yet still the seed of hope remains in children not yet grown,
If raised within a home with God, we'll never stand alone.
So, bless the homes whose quivers hold the promises of time,
For life is more than golden things, the elegant and fine.

PSALM 128: A BLESSING ON FAMILIES

Like vines entwined upon the tree they grow and flourish there,
The ones who fear and honor him who crafted every sphere.
Though hell itself launches assaults upon this family,
The fruit they bear is always there for all the world to see.

PSALM 129: SURVIVAL

Like fields deeply ploughed they were hunted and torn,
The furrows ran red where the lashes had scorned
The image of God the Creator of all,
Who lovingly caught every tear in a bowl.

Against them the enemy could not prevail,
For God cut the cords of the wicked with nails
Engraved on his hands and engraved on his feet
The names of the righteous reveal sin's defeat.

The scars they now carry are seeds for a world,
A world that is promised to bloom and unfurl
Into beauteous peace that we can't comprehend,
When sorrow and violence will come to an end.

PSALM 130: HOPE IN THE TRENCHES

From the depths of the trenches, I cry, and I scream,
dear God, set me free—set me free from the schemes
of the wicked who seeks to defeat and destroy
as he uses my sins and my faults to deploy
every tactic against me to come in between
my life and your love that is shown and is seen
in the wounds of my Savior, my King and my Lord,
that grant me forgiveness, my name to record
in the book of the living, the list of the free
and the ones who kept watching for what is to be.

PSALM 131: MY HEART IS NOT DIVIDED

I really am not superstitious, nor am I too ambitious,
I do not sit beside the high and lofty.
In matters great I'm not concerned, nor things profound, for I have learned
That in this life its better to speak softly.

For like a well-contented child, I know how to be meek and mild,
And satisfied with what you have decided.
For Lord you are my only hope, as I believe in what you wrote.
And I'm humble for my heart is not divided.

PSALM 132: THE ARK OF THE COVENANT

The storm-tossed king had vowed to build a place in which to serve
The Ark made of acacia wood in which there was preserved
The Tablets of God's Holy Law, the Manna, and the Staff,
But he was told his son would build the house on his behalf.

Yet it was he who took the Ark and brought it to the place
Where it would come to represent the Presence and the Grace,
But this was just an image of the Ark that was to come:
The Law, the Bread, and Staff was housed in God's own holy Son.

And now the Presence, not contained, but clothed in bone and breath,
A mercy-seat of sacrifice, enthroned in love and death,
Not carried now on poles of wood, but lifted on a tree,
The Ark once veiled in gold now shines in sacred mystery.

He bore the Law within his flesh, the Bread that satisfies,
And as the High Priest of our souls, he fully paid the price
Of sin and shame, of death and hell, so we are reconciled
With God and fellow humankind, the end of our exile.

The tomb was not his resting place, he gained the battleground,
Ascending to where cherubim in silent awe surround
The house that is unshakable, the city of our God,
Where Jesus reigns and mediates the covenant of blood.

PSALM 133: DEFINED UNITY

The psalmist praises unity as pleasant and as good,
But unity is founded on God's true and living Word.
There only is one loaf, one faith, one Savior, and one Lord,
Whose firm, commanding voice is like a sharp two-edged sword.

The precious oil that sanctified the tabernacle priests,
Is poured out on the ones who also celebrate the Feast.
Not just a balm for outward gifting of a group of men,
But calling back his creatures to submission once again.

The oneness of the Trinity defines our unity,
It is the dew that waters and restrains diversity.
We do not make this union bloom; it flows from God alone,
A gift descending with his grace, not something we have grown.

PSALM 134: COME AND LIFT UP

Come join the singing and jubilant crowd,
Come and make music and sing out aloud.
Come bless the one who made heaven and earth,
Come and adore him for all that you're worth.

Lift up your hands in the holiest place,
Lift up your eyes and see mercy and grace.
Lift up your hearts and sing worship and praise,
Lift and be lifted up now and always.

PSALM 135: NO GOD BESIDE THE LORD

No god can stand beside the Lord,
He made the sky; he shaped the land.
Clouds and lightning heed his voice,
The tempests fly at his command.

He does whatever he decides,
He rules the seas and lights the sky.
He's great, he's holy, and he's just,
So, he can never be defied.

He tears down tyrants from their thrones.
The proud who claim the world as theirs.
He lifts the lowly from the dust
And answers all his people's prayers.

These worldly doctrines let you down,
They sell you dreams that can't be found.
They promise peace, but bring no rest,
Just leave you empty, lost, and bound.

So, lift your voice and praise the Lord,
The one who knows your name by heart.
His love endures, his truth remains,
No lie can tear his work apart.

PSALM 136: I AM ASSURED

I looked at life and all I saw was bitter desolation.
All my dreams had failed, and I was left in isolation.
My hopes were slowly dimming as the sun fades from my day,
But even in the blackest night the stars can light our way.

Your words speak from the dawn of time and from them I can learn
That, while our circumstances may not always be transformed,
Your steadfast love remains the same and so it will endure,
For as you were with them you are with me, and I'm assured.

PSALM 137: SONG OF THE SOJOURNER

Like refugees living in sorrow and silence in lands not their own,
So, we are sojourning as pilgrims and aliens until we are home.
Our songs sing of sighing, of bleeding and dying, and longing for life,
So, how can we sing them while signs of our exile blot out our delight?

But in my locked spaces there still are the traces of victory won,
And I need correction through the resurrection of your blessed Son.
So, catch all the foxes, those bold paradoxes, that crowd out your voice,
And dash them in pieces as mercy increases my faith in your choice.

PSALM 138: PRAISE AND ADORATION

Out from the depths of poverty I look up to the sky,
And though I might feel quite alone and though I wonder why,
I know that you are walking with me each and every day;
I give you thanks, my sovereign Lord, and turn to you and pray.

You answered me and strengthened me, your purpose you fulfilled,
And while there may be troubled times ahead my fears are stilled.
Your steadfast love and faithfulness preserve my every breath,
Your power will prevail over all those who seek my death.

And while you may be lifted high, you bless the low and meek,
The haughty you resist because your love is quite unique.
The mighty rulers of this world shall see and they shall bow,
And they will turn to you, O Lord, in silence take their vows.

With all my heart I will give thanks, before the gods I'll sing,
Of praise and adoration for my sovereign God and King.
You are exalted far above the heavens and the earth,
And I believe that I will see creation's pledged rebirth.

PSALM 139: THE GOD WHO KNOWS ME INSIDE OUT

The one who knows all things beyond the outer rims of space,
Beyond the boundless galaxies where darkness has a face.
The movements of the furthest spheres, the sun, the moon, the stars,
Expressions of the cosmic mind's extensive repertoire.

And yet this God who shaped the vast infinities above
Has traced the details of my life with tenderness and love.
He knew me when my form was just a whisper in the dark,
And knows my story, every thought, and every question mark.

He sees the code that forms the core of every string of cells,
The circuits firing in my brain, the secrets they don't tell.
He knows the songs my memory sings when I'm alone at night,
The shadows I have buried deep, the fears I have to fight.

But there is nowhere I can go where he's not to be found,
In life and death, in height and depth, above or underground.
To him my darkness is as day, he knows my every move,
He holds me in his mighty hand, I shall not be removed.

Such knowledge is too wonderful, too great to comprehend,
Awake, asleep, behind, before, on this I can depend,
The God who knows me inside out and knows my heart and mind
Is he whose love and goodness simply cannot be defined.

So, search me, Lord, and know my heart and try my every thought,
And lead me in your everlasting way until you've brought
Me safely to the other shore through days you knew before,
Because your thoughts have always been that I must be restored.

PSALM 139: IN THE IMAGE OF HIS GLORY

Chorus
In Christ the glorious image of God is made anew,
Created in eternal love, his mercy shining through.
From dust he once had formed us, but now he sets us free,
The image of his glory we now are called to be.

You formed me in the secret place, with love beyond compare,
Your hands have shaped my inward parts, your presence everywhere.
Fearfully and wonderfully, your works declare your name,
And in your likeness, Lord, we come, your image to proclaim.

In Christ we change the tent of dust, the heavenly to bear,
Transformed by glory's radiant light, your likeness we will wear.
From glory unto glory, recreated by your hand,
Reflecting awesome beauty, we rise, in you we stand.

Chorus

If any one be found in Christ, a new creation shines,
The old has passed, the new has come, eternal love defines.
Crucified with Christ we live, no longer we but he,
Christ within, our hope, our joy, our glorious destiny.

Renewed and resurrected, and clothed in him we stand,
Created in his righteousness, reformed by his command
To transfer us from darkness to reign with him in power,
Reflecting now his nature as demons flee and cower.

Chorus and Outro
In the image of his glory, forever we will sing,
Redeemed by love unchanging, our Savior, Lord, and King.

And to his name be honor, and to his name be praise,
In the image of his glory, until the end of days.

Also based on Genesis 1:27; 1 Corinthians 15:49; 2 Corinthians 3:18; 5:17; Galatians 2:20; Ephesians 4:24; Philippians 3:21.

PSALM 140: THE CRY OF THE CORNERED HEART

They hunt me like wolves through a forest of whispering lies.
Their venomous teeth are like serpents that slither and slide.
They've laid all their traps in the path where my footsteps must fall.
Their breath is a poison that thickens the air like a wall.

Guard me, O Lord, from the plots of the wicked and vicious.
Keep me far from the cruel, the ruthless, the cold, and malicious.
Save me, protect me, and cover my head in the battle,
Confound all their planning as they plot and as they prattle.

O Lord, tear the mask from the faces of shadow and schemes!
Come break all the nets they have woven to shatter my dreams.
Uphold the poor heart that the vultures have circled in vain,
Let justice roll down like a river and wash out my pain.

You cradle the battered, you gather the scattered like seeds,
You fashion a haven from ashes and scars that still bleed.
The upright will stand in your light when the night is far spent.
O God, hold my soul to your chest till the darkness relents.

PSALM 141: SET A WATCH FOR MY MOUTH

The voice of the world is deceiving, it batters my mind,
A thousand demands, a million more promises primed.
They tempt me to speak and to win, to deceive and to shout,
To sharpen my tongue like a sword so to never lose out.

But Lord, set a watch on my lips as a guard at the gate.
Restrain me from crafting my words into hammers of hate.
Teach me to listen to hear, to be slow when I speak,
To carry your mercy in language that shelters the weak.

The battle's not distant; it rises again and again.
Ambition and pride and the craving to dominate friends.
I taste in my mouth the hot rush of a venomous phrase,
And only your Spirit can help me extinguish that blaze.

So, strengthen my soul like a rock that resists every wave.
Deliver my speech from the paths that the flatterers pave.
Let honesty temper my voice and humility sing,
And let every word that I breathe be approved by my King.

Let wounds from a friend be the balm that my spirit receives,
More precious than lies spun in silk by the one who deceives.
If truth cuts me open, then let it be wielded with grace.
I'd rather be struck by the just than be kissed by the base.

O save me from crowds that applaud when I trample the small.
Preserve me from praising the voice that would hasten my fall.
Surround me with brethren who dare to speak light to my night,
And shape me to treasure the wounds that are born out of right.

So, keep me, O Lord, when the nets of the wicked are spread.
When snares lie in wait for my feet in the places I dread,
And lead me on safely though thorns and deceptions abound.
Let my steps be secure in the way where mercy is found.

PSALM 142: MY SURE SECURITY

Like gentle rain, my weeping falls and soaks the thirsty ground.
I'm tired of relentless blows and enemies abound.
They make my life a misery and I feel so alone.
I have no refuge anywhere, my future quite unknown.

I only have your promises, but they remain enough.
They keep me steady on the way in times when things get rough.
The traps they lay are covered well, but you know where they hide.
The secret things are known to you, and you are by my side.

O hear my cry! O answer me, for I am crushed and torn.
Deliver me from cruel hands that mock and leave me worn.
They weave their lies, they dig their pits, their malice dark and deep,
But you can break these prison walls and free your frightened sheep.

For you remain my hiding place, my sure security,
My fortress and the one who still deals bountifully with me.
You will surround me with the righteous ones who know your name,
And I will find a place to rest and thank you for your grace.

PSALM 143: I AM YOURS AND YOU ARE MINE

Today the earth tilts underfoot; my life is blown astray,
While hunters ring me round about and scent my heart for prey.
They grind me into ash and dust with tongues like splintered bone,
And bolt me in a tomb of gloom, and I am left alone.

I summon back triumphant years, the wonders of your hand.
I trace your footprints through the seas, your rivers through the sand.
My soul, a cracked and thirsting field, cries out for you again,
O answer, Lord! My spirit fails like mist against the sun.

The cooing dove in warbling song awakens morning skies.
O let me hear of steadfast love before the daylight dies.
Shine out your face and lift my feet across the flooded plain.
Unlock these shackled limbs of mine and breathe me whole again.

Teach me to weave your will through all the tempests of my days.
Steer me by unseen compass points through labyrinthine ways.
You will destroy the enemy of my immortal soul,
For I am yours and you are mine and you will make me whole.

PSALM 144: HANDS TRAINED FOR WAR

I praise you, my stronghold, my God, who has taught me to battle and stand,
Who arms me with skill and with courage to do all the things he commands.
Whose faithfulness shields me like armor, whose mercy still meets all my needs,
Who steadies my foot in the field because his presence is guaranteed.

For what is my life but a whisper that fades at the fall of the day?
Like vapor on glass, a shadow at night, or a blade of wheat in the hay.
Yet still you reach down from the heavens to shatter the walls of the proud,
You draw me up out of deep waters and rescue me from scheming crowds.

O God, let your hand be my saving, for falsehood and lies fill the air.
The mouths of the wicked are honey and venom, their words are like snares.
Our fields are laid waste by their cunning, their power extremely bizarre,
Yet still we will sing of your goodness beneath all the wreckage and scars.

O grant us a world re-created where sons rise like trees in their youth,
Where daughters are beautiful pillars, adorned with the splendor of truth.
Where homes can be safe without plundering, and streets echo laughter and song,
Where no grief-stricken cry breaks the stillness, and every life is prolonged.

How blessed are the people you rescue, whose joy is to call you their Lord!
We live as the witnesses standing on ground you have already restored.
We fight with the weapons you give us: your Spirit, our prayers, and your Word,
Till all the kingdoms of darkness fall and bow at the feet of our Lord.

PSALM 145: A BETTER PART

I've lived a harder life than some, yet softer than the worst.
I've known the hunger of the soul but never dying thirst.
For in the quiet, aching years, I found a better part:
The Lord who feeds the humble and who mends the broken heart.

His greatness none can search or scale; his mercies never cease,
His wonders shine in every land, his whispers promise peace.
I'll speak of all his mighty works, the kindness he has shown,
And bless his name with thankful songs for I am not alone.

The Lord is great and merciful, his love will never cease,
He's slow to anger yet he leaps to grant to all his peace.
His goodness covers everything in earth and sky and sea
And miracle of miracles his love extends to me.

The proud may build their kingdoms and may fill their barns with gold,
But every tower breaks and falls, and every hand grows cold.
Yet you, O Lord, are sure and strong; your promises endure,
Your steadfast love upholds my days, your kingdom stands secure.

You lift the lowly from the dust, you catch the falling soul,
You draw the broken to your side and make the wounded whole.
Your open hand feeds every heart that calls upon your name,
Your nearness satisfies my soul, you listen, and you save.

O let my tongue be quick to sing, my bones be slow to tire,
Let every breath within my chest be fuel on holy fire.
For you are good beyond all thought, your glory has no end;
My King, my God, my heart's true home, on you I can depend.

PSALM 146: PRAISE THE LORD!

Chorus
Praise the Lord, O my soul, I will sing all my days!
While I breathe, while I live, I will voice out his praise!
From now till forever as our King he shall reign.
Praise the Lord, O my soul, praise his glorious name!

Let this be my witness, through the storms I endure:
For while I yet whisper, my praises are sure.
No ruler delivers, no human can save,
Their breath soon will falter, their plans be derailed.

But glad are the hearts that in quietness rest,
That trust in the Lord and are perfectly blessed!
Our God is forever upright, true, and kind,
A refuge for outcasts, a feast for the blind.

Chorus

He frees the oppressed and he feeds all the weak,
He raises the fallen, he strengthens the meek.
He watches the orphan, the lonely, the lost,
Provides for the widow no matter the cost.

The Lord will reign on from all ages to come,
From fathers to children, his faithfulness runs.
So, while I have breath and a song to employ,
I'll praise him in sorrow, I'll praise him in joy!

PSALM 147: WHO?

Who gathers the outcasts and builds with them a gathering place?
Who determines the number of stars and who names them in space?
Who sews up the hearts that are broken and who heals the wounded?
Who chooses the humble, but casts off the proud and deluded?

Who is abounding in power and whose greatness is treasured?
Who has understanding that goes well beyond what is measured?
Who covers the heavens with clouds and prepares rain for the land?
Who makes the grass grow on hillsides and feeds little birds by hand?

Who is not overly mindful of objects of power or pride?
Who is impressed with those who revere him and set self aside?
Who grants us protection and blesses our children in the streets?
Who makes peace in our borders and fills us with the finest wheat?

Who governs the seasons and makes the winter melt into spring?
Who orchestrates summer and autumn with vivid coloring?
Who gives us statutes and laws so that we might know how to live?
Who has loved us so that we might know what it's like to forgive?

Who then is broken that he has not spoken a word that has healed?
Who then can notice and stubbornly stand with lips that are sealed?
Who but his people should worship and sing out praise to the Lord?
Who but his people should worship and honor the God we adore?

PSALM 148: PRAISE HIM

Praise him, you heavenly canvas and star-punctured sky.
Praise him, you heights where the angels and archangels fly.
Praise him, you sun with your golden unquenchable flame.
Praise him, you moon in your cold, silver, whispering train.

Praise him, you stars flung like seeds in the furrows of night.
Praise him, you planets that spin in the pools of his light.
Praise him, you fishes and all that live under the sea.
Praise him, you deepening mist and you icy cold sleet.

Praise him, you mountaintops crowned with vestments of snow.
Praise him, you valleys where wild, unseen flowers still grow.
Praise him, you beasts of the forest and birds on the wing.
Praise him, you small, microscopic, invisible things.

Praise him, you children with eyes full of wonder and awe.
Praise him, you elders who help their imaginings soar.
Praise him, all nations and tongues from the east to the west.
Praise him, all people whom mercy and justice have blessed.

Praise him, you people he gathers from shadow and dust.
Praise him, you poor who have learned how to hope and to trust.
Praise him, you leaders and rulers of peoples on earth.
Praise him, you saints whom he saved and has given new birth.

Praise him, the Son who disabled the darkness with light.
Praise him, the King who has conquered and given us life.
Praise him, ascended beyond every throne and domain.
Praise him, the Lamb who now lives and forever shall reign.

PSALM 148: PRAISE HIM

Praise him, you satellites spinning in silence on high.
Praise him, you data streams singing through circuits of life.
Praise him, you morning alarms and the hum of the train.
Praise him, you cities of glass and you scaffolds and cranes.
Praise him, you children with chalk on the sidewalk at play.
Praise him, you streetlights that bask in the fading of day.
Praise him, you forests in lungs of the breathing machines.
Praise him, you broken things mended where hope can be seen.

PSALM 149: SING TO HIM A SONG

The rider dressed in blinding light, whose name is good and true,
With holy hosts as entourage, the saved and the renewed,
Two-edged swords are in their hands, the holy living Word
That speaks and brings to naught the things that darkness has preferred.

Our King of kings and Lord of lords takes pleasure in us all,
He gilds us with deliverance and in his hallowed halls
The godly make their joyful praises heard with music sweet,
With dancing melodies composed in regulated beats.

So, let us all with gladsome voices sing to him a song,
And may our godly gathering bring honor to the one
Who loves the world so that he gave his one and only Son,
And through his final sacrifice our victory has won.

Also based on Revelation 19:11–16.

PSALM 150: PRAISE THE LORD GOD

Praise the Lord God in his sanctuary,
Praise the Lord God for his excellency,
Praise the Lord God for his mighteous deeds,
Praise the Lord God for the Word he decreed,
Praise him with music, with trumpet and lute,
Praise him with tambourines and with the flute,
Praise him with cymbals, with strings, and with dance,
Praise him with every extravagance.

SONGS

WE STAND BEFORE THE SEA

We stand before the sea, dear Lord, we stand before the sea.
We see the dust behind us, we see our enemy.
All human ingenuity has failed to save the day
And in our hearts, we wonder, will Satan have his way?

Will we lie crushed beneath his heel, will hell victorious be?
Will hatred, strife, and bitterness still reign perpetually?
Will sulphurous fumes engulf us all and drag us down below
The surface of this swollen stream infested with our foe?

Stand, believer, stand and see salvation by God's hand.
The God who freed the Hebrew slaves and wind and waves command
Is still the God who was and is and is to come again.
His Spirit touches deep within and turns the hearts of men.

Come, Lord Jesus, come to us, you are our only hope,
The evil one walks through the land, binding with his rope
Those whose pain and suffering have given way to wrath,
Whose hardened hearts and conscience seared have led them down this path.

We plead the blood of Jesus Christ as covering for us all.
We plead for the angelic hosts to hearken to the call
To battle principalities to cast down every power,
And through our prayers may God once more become our mighty tower.

We are a mighty army, strong, and rank on rank we stand
With thousands and ten thousands of God's angelic band
In fiery chariots ready to march against the hoards
Of hell and of destruction to break their fiendish cords.

We stand before the sea, indeed, but firmly on the rock!
Our faith will lead us on again though others may us mock.
The one who spoke and all was made still speaks in healing words,
Your love and care will win the day and render hate absurd.

MY GREAT APPEAL

O sovereign and most holy God, engage my heart and find
It is alone your cause, not mine, that occupies my mind.
My great appeal is that you will bring in your kingdom blessed.
Set up your throne in every place where Satan's hoards may nest.

It is your glory that I seek and in it I rejoice.
Your honor and your majesty I praise with song and voice.
You are the one and only God and I your name adore.
I long that all may share our love and enter heaven's door.

Let sinners to your throne be brought and let them there find rest,
For only you can bring them in to lie upon your breast.
Accomplish great and wondrous things, for this is what you do,
And may the angels all rejoice as souls return to you.

And may you use me as you will and do as you see fit.
But, O dear Lord, promote your work and save them from the pit!
For in your holy word, I read, the gates of hell will fall
Before the forward moving Church, before the gospel call.

To bring great numbers to you Lord to see that glorious day,
When multitudes from every place walk on the narrow way.
'Tis my desire and my hope, and so, toward that end,
I give my labour and my life this broken world to mend.

In both my weakness and my strength, I pledge to serve your cause,
So, answer my request, my Lord, in spite of all my flaws.

PRAYER FOR PERSPECTIVE

Creator and Almighty God all good gifts come from you;
Life and breath and happiness, each step we take anew.
You guide and you advance our way as we walk hand in hand
With you throughout each day and night, 'tis you who make us stand.

Provider of both great and small, sustaining by your Word
Each aspect of creation, each creature and each bird.
Our senses of both sight and touch, of taste, of smell, of sound,
All beauty and all loveliness alone in you are found.

All comfort and all holiness, all grace and mercy we
Receive each morning from your hand, each day with constancy.
Reveal your glory—shine your light—so we may freely see
Our need of grace—our need of faith—to serve you willingly.

O Shepherd of the flock of Christ, tend to your feeble sheep;
Take us to pastures lush and green, to waters still and deep,
The valley we have entered in is dark and reeks of death;
Remove all trace of fear and doubt, revive us with your breath.

O fix our eyes on things above and not on things below;
A beatific vision grant us all—and make us know
You as you are, as reigning King—perspective give us Lord
So we might know your will alone is done here and abroad.

Benevolent you are and good and wise and merciful,
All righteousness, all majesty resides within you still.
The tempter comes to steal and kill and seeds of doubt to sow,
But we see Jesus's victory o'er enemy and foe.

And so, we redirect our gaze from darkness unto light
And know within our deepest heart that you have won the fight.
And by your Spirit, Lord, we plead, gift us a single mind
That, in the midst of hell itself, our peace in you we'll find.

A HYMN OF PRAISE

Breathe in the goodness of the Lord, breathe deep my troubled heart.
He watches over everyone; he never does depart.
Through thick and thin, through light and dark, through storms and through the rains,
The Shepherd leads, the Shepherd guides, and faithful he remains.

Chorus
O praise the Lord omnipotent.
O praise the Holy One.
O praise the Spirit immanent.
O praise the only Son.

Though dark clouds gather overhead, though energies are spent,
The King of kings and Lord of lords hears every sad lament.
He is the only one who can turn darkness into light.
His chariots, ten thousand strong, put enemies to flight.

Chorus

We trust that he who never sleeps will keep a watchful eye
And, in the silences of prayer, his presence will draw nigh.
Though heaven's gates from time to time may seem securely locked,
His name is still Immanuel and he will not be mocked.

Chorus

In spite of stress, in spite of strain, we look to him who reigns;
By faith we see, though all is dim, what minds cannot contain:
That day by day he still can work together for our good
The many things that life may bring, as only Jesus could.

Chorus

ALL I TREASURE, LORD, IS YOU

All I cherished, all I counted, fades before your boundless grace.
Every longing, every striving, finds its rest in your embrace.
You have cleansed my soul from darkness, washed me white in mercy's tide.
Now I stand in robes of glory, clothed in you, I'm satisfied.

Chorus
O to know you ever deeper! O to gain that matchless prize!
The upward call of God in Christ; I am yours and you are mine.

Chains were broken, sin was shattered, when you called and set me free.
You subdued beneath your scepter all the wicked things in me.
As the Shepherd leads his chosen, as the Door swings open wide,
So, I walk where you have called me, safe within the Crucified.

Chorus

Bread of Heaven, now my portion, feeding faith with living fire.
Still I thirst, yet find my filling, still I climb, yet rise up higher.
For the heights proclaim your glory, and the depths resound your name,
Till my soul, in love's perfection, sees you fully, face-to-face.

Chorus

Based on Philippians 3:8–11.

SHADES OF BABEL

They gathered there upon the plains, the goal was clear for their campaigns,
To build a tower and estate; to make their name forever great.
But heaven saw their vain design and polarized them all in time.
That tower crumbled into dust, and greatness turned to rot and rust.

Chorus
Yet shades of Babel still are found, wherever pride and sin abound.
If human greatness is the goal, then hell itself will seize control.

A pharaoh ruled in Egypt's land; he would not bow to God's command.
The plagues and then the mighty sea allowed the slaves to be set free.
A shepherd boy with sling and stone stood firm before a giant alone.
He did not come with spear or sword but in the name of God, his Lord.

Chorus
So, shades of Babel still are found, wherever pride and sin abound.
If human greatness is the goal, then hell itself will seize control.

A king who walked in prideful might declared his throne the highest height.
Yet driven mad, he wandered wild, by greatness he had been beguiled.
A feast was spread, the wine was poured, another king defied the Lord.
Yet writing shone upon the wall, and Babylon was doomed to fall.

Chorus

The Caesars thought that they were gods and murdered all who were at odds.
So, Jesus, too, was crucified; their pride and greatness nullified.
And many who resisted him drank from the cup filled to the brim.
Designers of their own demise, they joined the ranks of those despised.

Chorus

A charismatic man once said, to make his people great again,
A nation ruling banks, he claimed, must perish in his death campaign.
He built the camps, they thought it fine that millions perished by design.
The ashes rose, the world stood by, we turned away and closed our eyes.

Chorus

Yet silence rears its head once more as history repeats the score.
The guilt and shame we felt before will once more drag us to the floor.
O foolish leaders, sons of men, you build and burn and build again.
And yet the Judge who knows each name will cast the proud in burning flame.

Chorus and Outro
But one who sits enthroned above, whose name is great, whose name is love,
Will bring all Babels to their knees, as all will bow to his decrees.

Based on Genesis 11:1–9; Exodus 5:2; 14:27–28; Judges 9; 1 Samuel 15:12; 31:4; 17:8–50; Esther 3; Psalm 2; Daniel 3:16–28; 4:30–34; 5:2–30.

KEEP ON

Nothing waits for broken hearts as life keeps on rolling by,
    no matter if you're standing tall or living on the fly.
The sun comes up, the whistle blows, the day begins to grind,
    and no one stops to talk or ask what's going on inside.

They told us when we still were young that things would work out fine,
    that every road would lead us home, that we were meant to shine.
But life does not write fairy tales, nor stop to set things right,
    it drags you through the groggy day and haunts you through the night.

Chorus
But keep on walking, keep on breathing, even when you break,
    go step by step, don't turn around, there's too much here at stake.
For every tear and every trial, each stumble on the way,
    is proof you fought another round and lived another day.

I've worn a smile like porcelain when my spirit came undone,
    I've carried dreams on weary feet that never learned to run.
And though my hands are torn and worn from holding on too tight,
    I'll tie my shoes, I'll grit my teeth, I'll make it through all right.

The weight of time is heavy as it bends you, but won't break,
    it whispers lies that steal your hope, it tempts you with escape.
But somewhere in the trash heap of a life that feels too long,
    a quiet voice inside of you is humming one more song.

Chorus

So, here we stand, a ragged lot, but standing just the same,
    the battle scars upon our souls another claim to fame,

For all the times we could've quit, for all the times we stayed,
    for every time despair arrived but never got its way.

So, walk the road, no matter if it's paved in gold or dust,
    and when you're feeling hollow, when your bones begin to rust,
Just know that deep within you is a Fire that never dies,
    a whisper in the bitter wind that tells you to survive.

Chorus

GRACE AND GLORY

Child of mercy, rise in wonder, bathed in love's eternal glow.
Christ has called, his grace has claimed you, in his light you stand, made whole.

Chorus
Open our eyes to realms of glory, unveil the fire that lights the skies!
Fashion our hearts with holy splendor, kindle your radiance deep inside.

Endless thanks, O God of kindness, every breath a song of grace.
Faith unwavering, hope unshaken, held secure in love's embrace.

Chorus

Like the rivers feed the ocean, may our love stretch wild and free.
Rooted strong in truth unyielding, bound as one in unity.

Chorus

Bridge
Through the tempest, through the shadow, still your mercy guides us through.
Joy unshaken, hope unbroken, ever faithful, ever true!

Outro
Now to him whose power is boundless, far beyond our dreams and days!
Grace unmeasured, love unceasing, reigning now in endless praise! Amen!

Inspired by the prayers and benedictions of Paul: Romans 1:7; 15:5–6, 13; 16:25–27; 2 Corinthians 1:2; 13:14; Galatians 1:3–5; Ephesians 1:17–19; 3:16–21; Philippians 1:3–5, 9–11; Colossians 1:9–11; 1 Thessalonians 1:2–3; 2 Thessalonians 3:3–5.

NO SIGHT COMPARES

I have seen the golden sunrise, watched the mountains touch the sky,
Stood in fields of endless wonder, awed by eagles soaring high.
I have heard the roaring waters, felt the thunder shake the ground,
Seen the spheres like flames in heaven, awed by silence, stunned by sound.

Pre-Chorus
But when I look at you, I see; you crowned in beauty, robed in light,
An awesome vision, majesty, a brilliant and amazing sight.
Chorus
Come and see the King of Glory, seated on his royal throne.
Angels cry in endless worship, saints behold the Cornerstone.
Holy, holy, God Almighty, all creation sings his name!
Let our hearts be lost in wonder, for no sight compares to him!

I have walked through silent forests, breathed the fragrance of the rain,
Felt the hush of sacred stillness, sensed your presence call my name.
Who am I to stand before you, in your grandeur and your might?
Yet you draw the lowly nearer, clothed in mercy, dazzling bright.

Pre-Chorus
And when they look at you, they see; you crowned in beauty, robed in light,
An awesome vision, majesty, a brilliant and amazing sight.
Chorus

OUR ENDLESS HOME

In Christ, the old has passed away, we are his new creations.
God gave us all the ministry of reconciliation.
He calls us now to share his peace, proclaiming sins forgiven.
For he made him who knew no sin to pay the sentence given.

Chorus
Though earthly frames will waste away, our hope remains unshaken.
For Christ has built a home above to which we have been taken.
For when we leave this world behind, our life with him continues.
His Spirit is our guarantee and so we are encouraged.

For some, our gospel may be veiled, for those whose minds are blinded.
Yet he who spoke and called forth light, the truth to us entrusted.
Yet even so, this treasure shines, through cracked and broken vessels.
To show that this surpassing power belongs to God, not mortals.

Chorus

We are afflicted and oppressed, perplexed yet not defeated
Our previous ways have died with him, in him we're resurrected.
We know that all who live in him, in Jesus will be risen.
And so we preach what we believe that grace may not be hidden.

Chorus

Based on 2 Corinthians 4:1–18; 5:1–10; Hebrews 12:22–24.

I LONG TO KNOW YOU MORE

I've known you as the conquering King, the Lord of all, my everything,
The one who calms the winds and waves, the one who rescues and who saves.
I've known you as the cleansing tide that washed away my guilt and sin.
Your mercy flowed like rivers wide and by your blood renewed within.

Chorus
But now I long to know you more; I press ahead to reach the prize,
The upward call of God in Christ, for you have made me yours.
All else I held so dear before I count as loss compared to this,
To know the power of your life and share in all your sufferings.

I've known you as refining fire, a flame that purges and rewards,
Through every trial, you lift me higher, until my life's conformed to yours.
I've known you as the Shepherd's hand, that leads me through both night and day,
Through every storm, through shifting sands, your rod and staff have led my way.

Bridge
O make me like you, Lamb of God, in death, in life, in faith, in love.
Until that day when by your grace, I'll know you fully face-to-face.

Chorus

Based on Philippians 3:8–11.

THEN WE ARE STRONGER

We've all had those mountaintop moments, but life is not lived in the clouds.
Most of our days we are wandering out on the plains with the crowds.
But then there are those darker valleys, when we feel our life is all spent,
When, stumbling along in our blindness, we wonder where all our friends went.

Chorus
When we are down, when we are out, when we no longer know what life's about,
When we call on our friends, on whom we depend, then we are stronger.

When we are besieged by bereavement and hard pressed on every side,
Then we need our friends to surround us, our trusted companions for life.
The enemy prowls like a lion seeking those he may devour;
Alone we are prey to his cruelty, easily we're overpowered.

Chorus
When we are down, when we are out, when we no longer know what life's about.
When we call on our friends, on whom we depend, we are made stronger.

But two or more can help defend us, not one of us need be alone;
A friend is a presence forever, a comrade who'll never disown.
If one of us falls by the wayside, another can help us upright;
We'll run the long race to the finish, together we will win the fight.

Chorus

Based on Proverbs 17:17; Ecclesiastes 4:10, 12; 1 Peter 5:8.
Inspired by Knox, *Best of Friends*.

MY FAITH

It's five in the morning and most all around me are still fast asleep,
But here I sit low at your feet and the fellowship's sweet.
And you speak in whispers that silence the clamoring noise of the night,
That brings peace to my soul and makes me know that its all right.

Chorus
That I'm not consumed by the darkness around me and pain everywhere
Speaks truth to my innermost being and tells me that you are still here.
Your love and compassion, your faithful persistence brings light to my days;
And so, I wait calmly in hope you continue to guide me always.

And when I'm disheartened and know that I'm heading straight in for a fall,
Its then that your Word jogs my memory and helps me recall
That many before me had faith even though they did not understand,
And it's from them that I learn, all fulfills your command.

Chorus

And so, I surrender my will and my life and my times and my all,
Without reservation, in faith I will answer your call.
Take all of my burdens, take all of the things that I worry about
That I may delight in your will and be wholly devout.

Chorus

Based on Lamentations 3:22–23, 25–26.

FOXES IN MY VINEYARD

A summons sounds from blaring screens; I answer, and I scroll,
Bills must be paid while deadlines loom, and schedules weigh me down.
The constant noise outside and in, the beeps, alarms, and calls
While programs rise, demands are made, and I begin to fall.

Some things to file, and notes that breed, commands replace requests.
I document my own decay, I'm feeling dispossessed.
Regret unfurls its vampire wings; its talons tear my chest.
I cannot shut off racing thoughts and never come to rest.

Pre-Chorus
The little foxes run amok, disturb my life and peace;
Their tails have all been intertwined, and set ablaze, released.
And I'm Burning; Burning; Burning.
Chorus
I must escape and yet I'm trapped, my hopes and dreams fall short.
Desires fail to realize, why can't I just abort?
If I had wings, I'd fly away and hide myself forever,
I'm too fatigued to fight this fight and so I will surrender.

I know that I am quite distressed as there's no resolution,
And then there is the guilt within, an inner revolution.
The searing grief of friends whose son committed suicide,
My weariness has blunted me, my faith seems like a lie.

Reports of genocide stream in, of war, of rape, of theft.
My prayers don't seem to leave the floor, and I am quite bereft.
I'm unfulfilled and yet so blessed, am I so self-absorbed?
That I can't look beyond my pain and see my loving Lord?

Bridge
Yet even scorched, the embers breathe, and trepidation sways.
What if the fire's refining me, the dross thrown in the blaze?
What if this fragile piece of clay is destined to be whole?
What if this broken reed is mended under his control?

Pre-Chorus
Still little foxes run amok, disturb my life and peace;
Their tails have all been intertwined, and set ablaze, released.
And I'm Burning; Burning; Burning.
Chorus

Outro
If I had wings, I'd fly away and hide myself forever,
I'm too fatigued to fight this fight and so I will surrender.

Based on Judges 15:4; Psalm 55:6; Proverbs 13:12; Song of Solomon 2:15.

O MY CHILD, I CARE

Intro
Who has believed what they have heard, and have they understood?
God is not blind, he is not deaf, for where you stand, he's stood.

The deluge came, the terrors rose, and threatened to engulf,
Earth's pitiful inhabitants, the ravaged and the rough.
Where is the Lord in all this pain and does he even care,
Our overwhelming suffering, the grief that's everywhere?

The shrieking in the dead of night, the trembling in the day,
The stumbling of the weary heart, the dying and decayed.
The hopelessness, the bitterness, the mordant mockery,
But softly like the morning mist, his voice came on the breeze.

Chorus
You think I cannot understand, but, O my child, I do,
For where you walk, I, too, have been, and all because of you.
In life and death I bore your grief, and paid for every tear,
I know distress, abandonment, and how it feels to fear.

I was despised and cast aside by those who were my peers,
And I was tempted as you are and heard the devil's jeers.
My trial was a travesty, my torture was severe,
But I was pierced and I was crushed to cancel evil's sneer.

And like a lamb to slaughter led, I let them do their worst,
For willingly I gave my life to wash away the curse,
To take away the penalty that you can never bear,
So that in me you may have life, for, O my child, I care.

Chorus and Outro
Who has believed what they have heard, and have they understood?
God is not blind, he is not deaf, for where you stand, he's stood.

Based on Psalm 56:8; Isaiah 52:13—53:1-12; Matthew 26:38-39; Hebrews 4:14-16.

WHEN STONES ARE ROLLED AWAY

The floor is cold, the walls are bare, where once were beating hearts,
Their presence lingers in the cracks as candle stains on hearths,
Where once had blazed a happy tune while voices rose in song,
The stark and empty pulpit speaks of promises long gone.

My prayers feel like the sparks that fly from striking rocks for fire,
Without the kindling or the wood to yield what I desire.
But now the silence settles in the shadows of the room,
Where faith in God is little more than traces of perfume.

There was a time when there was life and light and lasting hope,
But like the ones encased in vaults beneath the floors of oak,
A deadly veil of unbelief now covers empty minds,
And like decay it rots away their trust and makes them blind.

Prosperity, material wealth, and ease of life erase
What once was gained from fellowship and faith and love and praise.
And yet they speak of emptiness, of loneliness they wail,
Depression and anxiety on epidemic scale.

An empty church with empty pews may speak of yesteryear,
And yet that spark without the fuel remains a presence here.
The prophet once was asked by God if dry bones still could live.
Its not by power, nor by might, but what the Spirit gives.

So, though my prayers like leaden feet lie heavy on the floor,
The Shepherd still is gath'ring in who enter by the Door.
For like a stream that changes course when waters force their way,
Just so will hearts be turned to him when stones are rolled away.

Based on Proverbs 21:1; Ezekiel 37:1–14; Zechariah 4:6; John 10:1–18.

THE MAKER'S HAND PREVAILS

Intro
Although he put eternity into the human heart,
We are not able to discern the end of what he starts.

I stand upon the precipice, but do I dare look down?
What will I see beyond the mists, what spirits will I rouse?
What lies behind the great unknown, and can that be explained?
And will that knowledge set me free, or will I be ashamed?

If I perhaps dare to descend into the yawning void,
Then would I find a better life than what I had before?
Or is there purpose in the course that I have yet to run,
A time to hold, a time to weep, a time to overcome?

Pre-Chorus
Although he put eternity into the human heart,
We are not able to discern the end of what he starts.
Chorus
The seasons turn, the rivers run, the Maker's hand prevails,
For though our world may shift like waves, his steadfast love remains.
For everything beneath the sun, he holds it all in place,
And what he does endures beyond the bounds of time and space.

A time to build, a time to break, a time for loss and gain,
A time to speak, a time to trust, a time for sun and rain.
From dust to dust all will return and though we build again,
The only things that will remain is what our Lord sustains.

I lift my eyes beyond the void and see the morning rise,
The Maker weaves his perfect thread through time that he supplies.

Though mysteries may cloud my path and reason fade from sight,
His wisdom stands, his justice holds, his mercy guides through night.

Pre-Chorus, Chorus, and Outro
Although he put eternity into the human heart,
We are not able to discern the end of what he starts.

Based on Ecclesiastes 3.

TO LIVE FOR MORE THAN ME

I don't know what the answer is at this dark point in time,
    but this I know, that for a while, we have believed the lie
that choices bear no consequence, that bonds can be unwound,
    that we can sever root from soil and still stand safe and sound.

We traded depth for ease of use, our friendships for a mask,
    believing screens could substitute for hands once held and clasped.
We let our children linger long in artificial light,
    and thought the natural world could wait, its wonders out of sight.

We shrugged at need and passed it by, left mercy to the few,
    convinced that others had the time while we had work to do.
We derided leaders, turned away, withdrew from every cause,
    and told ourselves the common good was simply fraught with flaws.

And also, in our sacred space, we asked for all but breadth,
    for comfort, not conviction, for diversion, not for depth.
We let our faith be weaponized, reduced to battle lines,
    and when the dust began to rise, we thought that this was fine.

But nothing's fine and never was, there always is a cost.
    Communities untended wilt, and trust once lost is lost.
Our faith, unless it walks and breathes, from dust returns to dust,
    And soon all our relationships are broken by distrust.

This world we live in, here and now, is not some twist of fate.
    It is the sum of what we've sown, our fears, our loves, our hates.
And if we wish to change the course, to mend, to build, to be,
    Then we must choose what we forgot: to live for more than me.

Inspired by Mark Clavier.

THE FIELDS OF WAR BEAR WITNESS

We walked along the muddy fields where thousands of men died,
    in Flanders where humanity, exhausted by the lies
Of national pride and unity, expansion and of wealth,
    fought on for what they had no clue, except to stop death's stealth.

All mercy seemed to hide its face, as truth and justice fled,
    while kings and rulers vowed their cause was worth the countless dead.
The trench lines stretched like gaping wounds upon the shattered land,
    and souls, once bright with youthful hope, lay buried in the sand.

Yet through the din of shrapnel's cry and terror's bitter breath,
    a whisper rose, a desperate gasp for peace and no more death.
Not might, nor wealth, nor fleeting fame, nor empire's hollow boast
    can shape the world in righteousness, nor gain what it has lost.

O God, when leaders use their might yet spurn the way of grace,
    the fields of war bear witness to the bloodstains on their face.
O how I long for mercy's song and justice to be heard,
    no lies corrupting evil hearts, nor lines of truth be blurred.

WHO WAS THIS MAN?

Who was this Man who so embraced the dust that is our frame,
And who took root in broken earth and came to take our blame?
And though he now is lifted up, he was a source of scorn,
For many saw him marred and scarred, beyond all human form.

Who has believed this sad lament and who has understood?
Though King of kings he was enthroned upon a cross of wood.
The world passed by with turned-away and proud, unseeing eyes,
Yet angels wept with strangled breath and shuddered at his cries.

He bore no form of majesty, that we should look at him,
He was a simple labourer whose life was bleak and grim.
He was rejected and despised, acquainted with all grief,
So, all who should have valued him were filled with unbelief.

Our cup he drained, our shame he wore like linen on his skin,
And every lash that tore his flesh unstitched the cloth of sin.
For he was pierced to bear the curse, an offering for guilt,
And by his blood we have been healed with every drop he spilt.

For we like sheep have gone astray and followed our own ways,
So, on his back, he bore our load, his love for us displayed.
For in his palms our names are carved, engraved indelibly,
On him was laid our chastisement, the pain that bought our peace.

Just like a lamb to slaughter led, he opened not his mouth,
For at his trial he spoke no word, surrendering legal ground.
Convicted as a criminal, considered as a curse,
And yet their deeds, by him conceived, would grant us all rebirth.

They planned to make his grave among the poor and the despised,
To cast away his mortal frame where flames and worms reside.
And yet in death, they took him down, and laid him in a tomb,
A sepulchre made for the rich, encased in spiced perfume.

For even though the wicked men who ruled upon the land
Had gathered to decide his fate, it was your mighty hand
That governed all pronouncements made because it was your will,
That through his bruising he would see your promises fulfilled.

Out of the anguish there would rise a gate to paradise,
Because he has defeated death through his own sacrifice.
He saw the end beyond the grave, the joy beyond the nail,
And like the spring breaks winter's grip, his victory prevails.

Now he who once was clothed in flesh, the one who once was crushed,
The man of sorrows, raised to life, now intercedes for us.

Based on Isaiah 49:16; 52:13–15; 53; John 10:17–18; Acts 4:27–28.

GOLDEN REPAIR

They walked with God in human form and called him Friend and Lord;
Their hands had touched the Bread of Life, and they had heard the Word.
And on the mountain they had seen his true transfigured light,
And with one voice they all rejoiced for he was their delight.

The night was full, their hearts were warm, the supper passed with grace,
Yet very soon, the waning moon saw flames of shame embrace
The rock who'd sworn he never would the Lord he loved disown,
But coals of fear burned through veneer and Jesus stood alone.

Before the morning sky was red the rooster's hymn was sung,
Its piercing notes broke through his pride and cursed his failing tongue.
Then turning from the pressing crowd, and weeping as he ran,
The waves of guilt crashed overhead and drowned the fisherman.

Did whispers pass in sobbing gasps that Sabbath day of dread?
Did Peter beg, "Don't tell the rest what I so plainly said"?
Could love still bloom where shame had grown like thorns around a tree?
Could grace rebuild a ruined heart and set the captive free?

But mercy walks through bolted doors, and guilt can't still its voice,
And so once more the humbled rock was challenged with the choice.
No thunder now, no swords, no boasts; just quiet burning eyes,
And via each affirming word, love hammered through the lies.

With tender words, Christ entered in where guilt had made its bed.
Three times the answer rose until repentant tears were shed.
The shattered jar of pottery, now mended with his grace,
Was stronger than it was before as brashness was displaced.

Remember then the gentleness of one we call the Lord,
When fellow friends with grievous faults lie shattered on the floor.
May we speak love into the cracks of those who are ashamed,
Instead of pride-filled haughtiness and angry words of blame.

And may we learn the loving art of mending shards of clay,
Of turning life's adversity to something we embrace.
A mended and resilient, yet a humble, wisened life,
The cracks that once spoke to our shame, now gleaming with his light.

Based on the Japanese art of repairing broken pottery known as kintsugi or kintsukuroi.

POETRY

FAREWELL

It was a good road, truth be told, a little rough at times,
    but I believe that it will not be rougher down the line.
What lies ahead is guaranteed by him who walks with me,
    for he's the one who went before, the one who holds the key.

I did not walk this road alone, though often none could see
    the one who braced my stumbling feet and kept me safe at sea.
And whether in the countryside or in the bustling streets,
    I knew that he was always there; our fellowship was sweet.

And now, my road winds to its close, but I have no regrets,
    for I have kept the course he set, I am in no one's debt.
What lies ahead beyond this life is clearer in my mind,
    for faith believes what can't be seen of where the path unwinds.

The purpose of my wandering was to share with every soul
    the grace of God in Jesus Christ who came to make us whole.
And now there lies in store for me the crown of righteousness,
    awarded to the ones who have received his graciousness.

And as I crest this final climb and gaze from where I stand,
    I see a place more beautiful than any earthly land.
I see the one who called my name, who walked the road with me,
    the one who gave his life for mine, in whom I have believed.

So, here I stand, one breath away from all my heart has sought,
    to live with him who with his blood my ransomed soul has bought.
I go in peace, the race is run, the battle fought and won,
    and now my road comes to an end, I know my journey's done.

Based on Acts 20:18–35; Romans 8:38–39; 14:8; 2 Corinthians 5:8, 14–15; Galatians 2:20; Philippians 1:21; Colossians 3:3–4; 2 Timothy 4:6–8.

DUNKIRK

Like stranded whales, the wreckage lies across the sandy flats,
    upon the beaches of Dunkirk, where tides and time combat.
These rusting hulks were meant to carry men from certain death,
    and yet their final exodus became their final breath.

THE WOVEN YEARS

We met in a season of empty hands,
    when the world felt like a field unharvested.
The African sky stretched wide, waiting for rain,
    and you were the drought-breaking shower I did not expect,
soft and certain, sinking into my skin,
    rehydrating, restoring, rehabilitating.

We learned to love in borrowed rooms,
    between the sighs of the hungry and destitute
and the trembling hands of refugees.
    We wrapped newborn hope in blankets
stitched from our own unraveling,
    never counting the cost.

I trace the lines of your face
    as if memorizing Scripture.
The quiet verses of your kindness,
    the Gospels of your self-sacrifice,
the Psalms of your patience,
    the parables of your touch.

Years gathered like leaves in the river,
    two sons rising from the current,
their love, tears, and laughter rippling across time.
    We held them, more precious than platinum,
not to keep, but to guide,
    not to own, but to send.
Now they have other hands to hold,
    their own tables to set,
their own beds to make,
    their own families to cherish and build.

And we are made richer by five bright new threads
    woven into the tapestry of our days.

Still, it is your voice that always calls me home,
    through the hush of evening light,
through the urgent bustle of every day,
    and I turn to find you,
the beating heart amidst these woven years,
    the single thread that has never frayed or broken.

Love has never been a ledger between us,
    never a balance or scale,
only the steady offering of everything,
    the pouring out and the filling again.
What has been given will never be lost.
    What has been shared will never be spent.

And so together we enter the future,
    shoulder to shoulder, heart to heart,
wound to wound.
    We are, and always will be, two servants who found
that, in giving, the only love
    that asks for nothing, returns as everything.

To my wife, Louise, my beating heart amidst these woven years.

SILENCE IS THE LOUDEST GRAVE, WHEN PEACE LIES IN A SHROUD

The words were sharp as winter's wind and cut too deep to heal,
    a moment's wrath, a glance misread, the breaking of a seal.
The bridge we built with years of trust lay smouldering in the dust,
    for neither one would bend to mend, though mend it both we must.

A husband turns, a wife withdraws, a rift begins to spread,
    a home that should be warm with light is cold as if long dead.
An angry voice, a child estranged, a door that will not yield,
    a sour word, a letter burned, a bitterness congealed.

We once were brothers, blood and soul, what tore us both apart,
    what came between, what poisoned minds, what savaged bleeding hearts?
What once was light, grew dark with doubt, as love gave way to pride,
    and coldness spread like creeping frost, and kindness slowly died.

Now echoes haunt the awkward rooms where laughter used to ring,
    the one who waits for words unsaid has nothing more to bring.
And though we meet, the walls remain, agreements torn in two,
    and friendships that had shaped the world dissolve like morning dew.

We stand upon the fields of war where battle lines were drawn,
    where fathers fell and sons were slain for things they had not known.
What might have been, what should have been, no grave can tell us now,
    for time will not rewind the past, nor pride remake a vow.

Yet time has worn the bonds we built; the trust we held has thinned,
    and now our banners, once entwined, wave tattered in the wind.
We view old friends as parasites, and break the rules of trade,
    forgetting all the debts we owe, the sacrifice once made.

O nations weighed with power and might, remember what was lost,
  no war of words, nor cold disdain, is worth the final cost.
For time moves swift, and soon we'll find, too late, too blind, too proud,
  that silence is the loudest grave, when peace lies in a shroud.

STOP THE FRIENDLY FIRE

The night is thick with battle smoke, the air is sharp with cries,
Our foe is laughing in the dark, with malice in his eyes.
The ground is scarred with broken lines where once we stood as one,
But friendly fire's blown apart all what we once had won.

And yet this is no battlefield, not in the usual sense,
This is the Church of Jesus Christ with razor-wired fence.
We claim that we're all sinners, saved solely by his grace,
And yet we judge and crucify the ones we should embrace.

Our house is shaking, walls are cracked, our pews are split in two,
We swore to stand as living stones, but is this what we do?
The light of Christ was meant to shine, yet smoke is all we see,
For friendly fire's choked the air where grace and love should be.

We speak of truth but hurl our words like sparks upon the wind,
We brand each other heretics; the real deceiver grins.
We fight for scraps of strategy, for doctrines, means, and lines,
Forgetting that not one of us is perfectly aligned.

A house divided cannot stand; the wise don't torch their own,
And yet the deepest wounds are those that come from friends we've known.
We call it right, we call it brave, to tear down and expose,
And while we fight amongst ourselves, the kingdom will not grow.

So, let the wounded bind the wounds of all within his fold,
Lay down our arms of fear and pride, in graciousness be bold.
For if we bleed each other dry, what victory remains?
The gospel wilts in barren soil where mercy dies in flames.

A SPRING WALK IN THE DUNES OF SCHOORL

The dunes rise high where restless winds have shaped them through the years,
    their creamy sands, like sifted light, still damp from misty tears.
The sky, a burnished steel-blue sheen, spreads wide above our heads,
    with scraggly pines on sandy slopes, their writhing roots outspread.

The whispering breeze bears salty scents from seas concealed beyond,
    its thin cold voice breathes through the pines as if to correspond.
The moss glows bright in emerald flames, the ivy clings in shade,
    while snowdrops star the gentle hills where winter's shadow fades.

A thousand greens in shifting hues where shrubs and heather sprawl,
    some holding close their hidden buds, some greyed as seasons call.
The ferns still bear the curling scars of frost's retreating hand,
    yet life unfolds in quiet grace upon the breathing land.

The pools lie dark where waters rest in brackish, glassy sleep,
    reflecting birch in silent thought where mallard ducklings keep.
And high above among the pines the sweet songs of the birds
    do not disturb the sacred hush that speaks yet without words.

Some climbs are steep, some sand is deep, each step a straining test,
    but cool the air and sweet the breeze that fills our labouring chests.
Yet as we walk the whisper comes, more striking than the view:
    "Be still, my child; this path is mine, and I am here with you."

YOUR STREAMS FLOW IN THE WILDERNESS

The dunes seem higher than they were when I was very young,
  each step I take, the liquid sand sinks back from where I've come.
The wells of water, far apart, my soul is parched with thirst,
  and when I think I've faced it all, things seem to get much worse.

Mirages keep misleading me in thinking I've arrived,
  the blazing sun is merciless, and I am quite surprised
that I have not been overcome by life's relentless rush,
  nor has my heart been pulverized nor has my soul been crushed.

But as I crest another height, I see far down below
  a fountain flowing steadily, and suddenly I know
that you have not forsaken me and that I need not fear,
  for you are with me personally when all seems most severe.

Your streams flow in the wilderness, your springs rise from the dust,
  the searing, burning torch of trials, the gnawing of the rust,
Are tools held in your master hand to shape what I must be,
  for only in my levelling am I made more than me.

Yet in the furnace of your will, my soul is not destroyed,
  for in the ashes I am forged, and dross is burned and void.
The wastelands blush with cedar trees, with myrtles green and wide,
  and rivers run where once my life was cracked and scorched and dried.

So, though the dunes rise high ahead, I climb without despair,
  for every step is measured by your love and endless care.
And when I reach the farthest crest, beyond what I can see,
  I'll find the wells you promised, and I'll drink abundantly.

Based on Psalm 23; Isaiah 41.

SANCTIFICATION

Wave after wave of relentless love
    keeps washing over my shadowed heart,
Carving away at the cliffs of stone,
    crafting from pieces a work of art.

Ploughing through hardened and fallow ground,
    clearing the way for sower and seed,
Flowing sweet waters gently and swift,
    healing the memories that still bleed.

Cradled in hands once broken and torn,
    swept by a wind that is warm and strong,
Led by a whisper that drowns out noise,
    hushed by a knowledge of where I belong.

Seated in places where angels reside,
    clothed in a radiant robe of light,
Filled with a breathing and living love,
    lavishly fed by the Bread of Life.

HOW THE VAN DER BIJLS GOT THEIR NAME

The winds of Egmond howled that night through forests dark and deep,
    as fearless Wouter, chained in steel, resigned to fate and sleep.
A jealous count, through trickery, had captured him that day,
    and there beneath the castle's weight, Wouter began to pray.

Four brothers stood in Egmond's halls, their loyalty unyielding,
    their hands were strong, their heads were clear, their rescue plans
    conceiving.
They swore before the chapel's cross, by blood and by their kin,
    that Wouter would not die in chains; they would deliver him.

Through frozen marsh and moonlit fields, their whispered steps were fleet,
    with axes sharp and hammers raised, they vowed none would retreat.
The moat lay black, the walls loomed high, the guards stood stern and tall,
    yet as they crept, a mist arose and wrapped them in its shawl.

With Jan the Axe, first through the gate, his blade like lightning fell,
    it split the iron, bit the wood, there was no time to yell.
Cornelis struck with hammer's might, the echoes shook the night,
    while Pieter swung his mighty club and sent their foes to flight.

Through blood and fire, steel and stone, they reached the prisoner's keep,
    and Jacob leapt into the cell where Wouter lay asleep.
"Awake, my lord! The night is ours! You are no more confined!"
    With thankful heart, the count arose, delivered just in time.

They fled before the morning drum, through shadows, smoke, and flame,
    and Wouter swore the brothers would live on in noble fame.
"No braver men have I beheld in peril or in war,
    and so, by right, your names shall stand in honor evermore!"

Then Jacob took "van Kamer" proud, for first into the room,
    and Jan was given "van der Bijl," his axe saved them from doom.
Cornelis bore the "Klopper" name, the hammer in his hand,
    while Pieter, called "van Codde," stood; a club was his command.

And so, the name was forged in fire, in battle, blood, and grace,
    a gamekeeper turned noble knight, the axe, his sword in place.
Through centuries the tale was told, through war and peace the same,
    and still the wind of Egmond sings the name of van der Bijl.

A LESSON WE MAY NEVER LEARN

I hear the whispers of the trees here in the Delville Wood,
    they speak in silence, but tell more than our words ever could,
Of fearsome cries, of fatal fumes, of burning pits of oil,
    for they drink deep of death and hate; of blood soaked in the soil.

We walk between the granite stones that mark the graves of boys
    who could have served humanity and lived their lives with joy.
But here they lie beneath the ground that serves to speak for them
    a lesson we may never learn; therein we stand condemned.

For yet there was a Second War; a shameful, sad repeat,
    where wreckage screams of evil deeds that made all heaven weep.
And dotted over countrysides, the graves of countless dead,
    in words of desperate vigilance, warn us to look ahead.

But do we stand upon the edge of yet another war?
    It seems the war to end all wars has taught us nothing more.
And narcissistic tyrants rise, as many have forgot
    the bitter tales that lie interred beneath the rotting sod.

Based on poems written by my maternal grandfather, John Lomax, in his published work *Songs of Strife*.

THE BALLAD OF THE NEW CREATION

Before the voice that summoned light, there was a formless deep,
The Spirit brooded over all in silent hovering sweeps.
The darkened void hung motionless until the Word unseen
Spoke into being all that is and all that is to be.

Then broke the darkness into light, an evening and a day,
The Cosmic Artist sung the stars and laughed the Milky Way.
He spun the world in rhythmic turns of sky and sea and earth,
He breathed into a lump of clay and granted Adam birth.

The pinnacles of what he made were called to represent
The one whose image they revealed, and they were quite content.
Then on the seventh day he ceased; he finished all he'd made,
He hallowed it and rested from the goodness now displayed.

But then the serpent found the tree and coiled it with deceit,
And in the garden sin destroyed the fellowship once sweet.
A woman stood beneath the tree as God looked on and cried,
The precious jars of clay he'd made lay shrivelled, cracked, and dried.

Yet mercy wove within the curse a thread of golden grace:
Broken, not discarded shards of pottery, though defaced,
Would once more be re-storied, in renewal beautified,
As he reversed the dreadful curse that day when death would die.

Again, the Spirit brooded, not over waters, but the womb,
And so was born the Holy Child in brokenness and gloom.
The Word once more spoke light into the world that he had made,
And yet the serpent coiled again, and Jesus was betrayed.

There on the cross the darkness clashed with Word and light again.
"It's finished," the Creator cried as life came to an end.
The women stood beneath the tree, as God looked on and cried,
His precious incarnated Son bowed low his head and died.

Again, the seventh day was still, the Creator was at rest.
He'd robbed the grave of victory and raided Satan's nest.
But then the Spirit moved once more, once more the voice was heard,
The rising, swelling, upsurge of the symphonic living Word.

Still, shards of broken pottery we all appear to be,
But as the wounds that bought us life, still there for all to see,
Were not removed nor were replaced, but borne and deified,
So are our cracks with glory filled, renewed and beautified.

He does not cast the world aside, though shrivelled, cracked, and dried,
But gathers shards of shattered clay and with what he supplies
Creates a new yet better work of art that will reveal
The love of God that shines so clearly through the wounds he heals.

THE BALLAD OF THE THIEF

I've walked the corridors of doubt where silence claws the soul,
Where night won't lift, and voices shout from caverns black and cold.
I've tasted shame that stings like fire that burns the breath from prayer,
And still, although I've looked up higher, I found no comfort there.
Yet here, this place of ash and bone where justice has no name . . .
I bleed beneath a sky of stone and only I'm to blame.

But him . . .

No myth, no metaphor, no dream, no whisper from the deep,
But here he cries a primal scream, and I begin to weep.
The evil etched in every face now stared from mine as well.
It wasn't just the world's disgrace; my life was but a shell.
I saw the shadow I'd become, the self I couldn't hide . . .
The fist that strikes, the heart gone numb, the love I crucified.

And yet amid that savage day, that hour devoid of grace,
He turned to one who'd lost his way and looked me in the face.
No list of virtues to defend, no past to recommend . . .
Just me, condemned. And yet, my end I could not comprehend.
He did not speak of what I'd done, he named no wound or vice.
He simply said, "This day, you'll come with me to paradise."

WHERE YOUR FOOTSTEPS FALL

Our home is full of echoes now, the softest kind of sound,
The whisper of your laughter in the spaces all around.
Your footsteps walk a distant road beneath another sky,
And though I smile for you, my love, I wish you were nearby.

We've weathered storms and wars and griefs, and still our hearts beat true,
Each scar we bear, a testament to all that we've come through.
Now every breath you take out there, each prayer, each rising sun,
Reminds me that I'm missing you, though you and I are one.

I miss the way your eyes light up when sunlight strokes your hair,
The simple things, the quiet things, the way you fill my air.
The way you hold our broken days as gently as a sigh.
The world is vast, but you, my love, are still my lullaby.

So, walk your miles, and sing your songs, and let your spirit soar.
I'll keep the watch, I'll keep the flame, I'll love you even more.
And when your journey leads you home, I'll meet you in my heart,
A pilgrim's soul, a lover's arms, together not apart.

To my wife as she walked the Camino de Santiago with her sister.

ODE TO THE BUTTERCUPS IN THE FIELD

You bloom where no one thinks to look; in fields where herbage grows,
A scatter of unspeaking stars where peace and quiet flows.
No gardener boasts your pedigree, there are few who know your name,
Yet morning bends to kiss your face as breezes sway your frame.

The mighty speak in marbled halls, their voices loud and long,
They revel in the spotlight of their captivated throngs.
But you, content with cloistered roots, in wordless worship stay.
You gild the field with gratitude and teach us how to pray.

The ones who pass you do not know what quiet work you do.
How in your sweet simplicity you make us see anew
The grandeur of the one who made your intricate design,
God's glory shining silently through holy golden shrines.

O Buttercups, you preach to me; while greatness goes to seed,
God walks among the small and bright and crowns the lowly weed.

THE MAN IN THE MIRROR

I looked in the mirror and saw not a face, but a field that was plowed,
Furrowed and weathered by years of endlessly seeking to please the crowds.
My soul has grown calloused from tirelessly building the dreams of the blind,
My back is a ledger of burdens I carried for those who have left me behind.
They called me a good man, and maybe I was, but what has it cost?
I gave them my daylight, my marrow, my strength, but now it's all lost.
I lie down to sleep, but my thoughts are relentless and won't leave me alone,
While I'm praying for quiet, for pasture, for water, for rest, for a home.

I've labored in vineyards that weren't even mine, just because it felt right.
Fed mouths that forgot me and fought for things that were never my fight.
They said I was noble, a pillar, a rock, a reliable man.
But pillars grow weary when no one remembers to tend where they stand.
I've smiled through betrayals, kept silent through falsehoods and let them all pass;
But silence is heavy and finally settles like silt in my glass.
I'm tired of the striving, the hustle, the virtue that burns at my soul;
O Shepherd, please lead me where stillness and mercy will make me whole.

Last night I lay still on my bed in the dark till the dawn nearly broke,
No prayers on my tongue, just the weight of the world hung like a heavy cloak.
And something within me gave way, like the crack of a branch in a flood,
Not broken or snapped, but released in the swell of a mercy-soaked mud.
From a place deep within me I knew I had no more to give; I was done.
But the silence that answered was warmer than the rays of the sun.
Not a voice, not a vision, but a presence, like fresh breath in my chest,
Like someone had gathered my shards and my fragments and given me rest.

So, let the world carry its ledgers, its ladders, its endless scores;
I've climbed them enough to know that they won't open any right doors.
I'd rather lie down by the water on grass where my Shepherd still sings
And trust him to guard me from lesser and darker and lonelier things.
He leads me along by a way I never could earn on my own,
And makes barren deserts and even wastelands feel strangely like home.
I'm trading my striving for stillness, my pitiful plans for his pace,
And I'm hoping to find, in the quitting, the first true breath of grace.

The bills will still come, and the nights will still be heavy with anxious thoughts;
Nothing will change, and the wars and the battles I face will not stop.
But now, when I shoulder the load, I know I'm no longer alone.
He's here by my side, a presence that's with me until I get home.
He walks where I walk, through the heartbreak, the noise, the haze, and the ache.
Not lifting me out, not picking me up but giving me strength not to break.
I don't need to escape; I need him to make and to help me believe:
That even here in my sorrow, there's peace I can finally receive.

Dedicated to my great-grandfather who, despite working hard, establishing schools, colleges, planting and building churches in Mauritius and South Africa as an Anglican missionary, clergyman, and schoolmaster, struggled most of his life to feed and clothe his family of ten. Also, to the many missionaries who have been forgotten by those who sent them and those who received them.

Bibliography

Ayres, Pam. *The Works: Selected Poems*. London: BBC, 2005.
Bowie, John. *Walking Towards the Noise*. Bristol Noir, 2022.
Brown, J. G. *Verse for You, Book Three: A Collection of Verse for Senior Forms*. Cape Town: Longmans Southern Africa, 1975.
Browning, Elizabeth Barrett, and Robert Browning. *Love Poems of Elizabeth Barrett Browning and Robert Browning*. New York: Barnes & Noble, 1994.
Chapman, Michael, ed. *The Paperbook of South African English Poetry*. Parklands, S. Africa: Donker, 1986.
Coleridge, Samuel Taylor. *The Works of Samuel Taylor Coleridge*. Ware, UK: Wordsworth Poetry Library, 1994.
Cotter, Jim, compiler. *Etched by Silence: A Pilgrimage Through the Poetry of R. S. Thomas*. Norwich, UK: Canterbury, 2013.
Donne, John. *John Donne: Poems*. Edited by Hugh I'Anson Fausset. London: Everyman's Library, 1976.
Dylan, Bob. *The Lyrics: 1961–2012*. New York: Simon & Schuster, 2016.
Fergusson, Margaret, et al., eds. *The Norton Anthology of Poetry*. 6th ed. New York: Norton, 2018.
Fujimura, Makoto. *Art + Faith: A Theology of Making*. New Haven: Yale University Press, 2020.
———. *Silence and Beauty*. Downers Grove, IL: IVP Books, 2016.
Guite, Malcolm. *David's Crown: Sounding the Psalms*. Norwich, UK: Canterbury, 2022.
Hudson, Grant P., ed. *Poetica #22: An Inner Circle Writers' Group Poetry Anthology*. Sheffield, UK: Clarendon House, 2025.
Knox, Phil. *The Best of Friends: Choose Wisely, Care Well*. Downers Grove, IL: IVP, 2023.
Lawrence, D. H. *Selected Poems*. Edited by Keith Sagar. Harmondsworth, UK: Penguin, 1975.
Lomax, John. *Songs of Strife*. Durban, S. Africa: Davis & Sons, 1918.
Longfellow, Henry Wadsworth. *Selected Poems*. New York: Penguin, 1988.
McCann, J. Clinton, Jr. "Psalms." In *1 & 2 Maccabees; Introduction to Hebrew Poetry; Job; Psalms*, 639–1280. Vol. 4 of The New Interpreter's Bible. Nashville: Abingdon, 1996.
Mitchell, Kevin M. *Essential Songwriter's Rhyming Dictionary*. Los Angeles: Alfred Music, 1996.
Poems of the Great War: 1914–1918. London: Penguin, 1998.

Smith, Geoffrey Bache. *A Spring Harvest: A Collection of Poetry*. Edited by J. R. R. Tolkien. London: Magna Liborum, 2022. First published in 1918 by Erskine MacDonald.

Studdert-Kennedy, G. A. *The Unutterable Beauty: The Collected Poems of G. A. Studdert-Kennedy, Otherwise Known as "Woodbine Willie."* Cornwall, UK: Diggory, 2006.

Verleyen, Herwig. *In Flanders Fields: The Story of John McCrae, His Poem and the Poppy*. Translated by Bertin Deneire and Ian Connerty. Koksijde, Belg.: De Klaproos, 2002.

Wright, Franz. *God's Silence*. New York: Knopf, 2006.